The Epigram

in the

English Renaissance

The Epigram
in the
English Renaissance

by Hoyt Hopewell Hudson

1966
OCTAGON BOOKS, INC.
New York

Reprinted 1966
by special arrangement with Princeton University Press

OCTAGON BOOKS, INC.
175 FIFTH AVENUE
NEW YORK, N. Y. 10010

LIBRARY OF CONGRESS CATALOG CARD NUMBER: 66-18047

Printed in U.S.A. by
NOBLE OFFSET PRINTERS, INC.
NEW YORK 3, N. Y.

◄ FOREWORD ►

Hoyt Hopewell Hudson died suddenly at his home in Palo Alto, California, on June 13, 1944, in his fifty-first year. His unexpected passing brought a keen sense of personal loss to all who had experienced directly the warmth of his friendliness, the breadth and humanity of his learning, and the interest and eagerness with which he would always aid a colleague who was struggling with some intractable problem.

To American scholarship Hoyt Hudson's death has brought a loss no less grievous—one that will be deeply felt by that even wider circle of friends who had become acquainted with him through the books and articles he had published. All students of sixteenth- and seventeenth-century poetry are familiar with the volume of *Poetry of the English Renaissance* that he edited with J. W. Hebel, an anthology designed for classroom use which was at the same time, both in text and notes, a work of distinguished scholarship. The standard that this book set in 1929 became the measuring rod with which all later volumes of this sort have been appraised. Scholars of the Renaissance are indebted to Hudson for the studies of rhetoric and poetry which led to his edition of John Hoskins' *Directions for Speech and Style*, to his translation of Erasmus' ironic encomium *The Praise of Folly*, and to a number of essays in scholarly journals and in the volumes honoring James Albert Winans and Alexander M. Drummond. Yet his interests, nurtured in his years as a graduate student at Cornell University, ranged beyond the period of the Renaissance and carried him into the larger subject of the history and theory of rhetoric—the disciplines which give academic substance to the training of the teacher of public speaking. As a scholar and teacher of literature, he was deeply concerned about the confusion in aims and methods of contemporary education. A student of poetry, he was himself a poet.

[v]

These varied activities of scholar, teacher, and poet are reflected in the three books upon which Hoyt Hudson was engaged at the time of his death. He had almost finished selecting and arranging a group of his poems for publication. The volume was issued in 1945 by the Grabhorn Press in San Francisco with the title *Celebration*. At the same time he was a little past mid way in the writing of a treatise concerned with liberal education. Entitled *Educating Liberally*, the fragment was published by the Stanford University Press. Much farther from completion than the other two, the manuscript for a third book, *The Epigram in the English Renaissance*, consisted of only three chapters and part of a fourth in finished form. These chapters, probably less than a quarter of the book that the author had intended, make up the present volume.

Those who knew Hoyt Hudson were aware that he looked forward to making his book on the English epigram the most notable scholarly work of his career. His Cornell dissertation, submitted in 1923, had been on "Elizabethan and Jacobean Epigrams." Throughout the twenty-one years that followed, in the midst of other tasks, he assiduously collected further material on the subject, to the end that his book, when finally completed, should not fall short of his scholarly ideal of a truly comprehensive study, resting securely upon a survey of all available evidence. His year as a Visiting Scholar at the Huntington Library in 1934 gave his further research its greatest impetus. Shortly thereafter, apparently, drawing upon his riper knowledge and vastly augmented notes, he set about rewriting the earlier chapters of his dissertation. He had progressed as far as the middle of Chapter IV when other duties intervened. After his death these four chapters, each in a separate folder, were found among his papers. The first three folders he had marked "Finished"; the fourth, in addition to a manuscript in final form for the first part of the chapter, contained several rough, unannotated drafts for later paragraphs. The vast collection of notes for subsequent chapters demonstrated that the author's plan called for a far more extensive revision and augmentation of his 1923 manuscript for this section of his work than for the earlier portions. Unfortunately, these notes had not been arranged in a way that another could make use of them. Only by consulting the author's Cornell dissertation can one gain a notion—though a very imperfect one—of the design and contents he had in mind for the remainder of the book.

Even though only a small portion of *The Epigram in the English Renaissance*, as Hoyt Hudson had planned it, was in shape for publication, it seemed to some of his friends that the fragment should be examined carefully to see whether it might not be possible to publish it. An informal committee, consisting of Professors W. S. Howell of Princeton University, Everett L. Hunt of Swarthmore College, and Francis R. Johnson of Stanford University, undertook the task, and when Princeton University Press decided to publish the work, agreed to see it through the press.

Our editorial policy has been to print the manuscript just as the author left it, restricting our labors to supplying one or two missing references, and to reading the proofs. Knowing that Hoyt Hudson, had he lived, would certainly have given the manuscript a further revision and polishing before turning it over to the printer, we have an uneasy feeling that we may be doing him a disservice by publishing a work that he did not consider entirely ready for the press. We console ourselves with the belief that we would do him a greater disservice by not publishing it at all.

The chief burden of the reading of proof has fallen upon Mr. Howell, although Mr. Hunt and Mr. Johnson have each checked a copy of the galleys. Mrs. Hudson has prepared the index. For any errors that we have failed to detect, we jointly assume responsibility. We hope there will be few; should there be many, we are confident that the author, who was ever tolerant of the shortcomings of his friends, would have been our most indulgent reader and critic.

F. R. J.
W. S. H.
E. L. H.

 CONTENTS

*Ainsi ie pouray instruire les foibles, & con-
firmer les forts, dans la gaye & agreable
Science de l'Epigramme.*

COLLETET, *Traitté de l'Epigramme* (1658)

CHAPTER I · THE NATURE OF
THE EPIGRAM

"THE epigram is a witty kind of writing—though not all who write it are witty," says the Latin motto which a seventeenth-century epigrammatist placed upon the title page of his book. By the same token, not all of the scores who, during the past four hundred years, have commented upon the nature of the epigram can be termed epigrammatic commentators. The subject seems to have been a favorite one with our ancestors; and a few excerpts from their disquisitions upon it will be found in this chapter. Of late years a tone of discouragement has here and there crept into "la gaye & agreable Science" of M. Colletet. "Nothing could be more hopeless," states the writer of the article "Epigram" in the *Encyclopedia Britannica* (eleventh edition), "than an attempt to discover or derive a definition wide enough to include all the vast multitude of little poems which at one time or other have been honored with the title of epigram, and precise enough to exclude all others." Gayley and Kurtz echo this: "The variety of poems termed epigrams is so vast as to defy satisfactory classification according to either content or form."[1] To one attempting a survey of the epigram in Elizabethan England these warnings might well hold special terrors. Writers of the sixteenth century frequently seem to us most careless in their use of literary terms. We recall that the word "sonnet," now so clearly defined to every reader of poetry, was placed over poems of all lengths up to thirty or forty lines and of almost

[1] *Methods and Materials of Literary Criticism* (New York, 1920), p. 30.

any metrical pattern. We shall not expect to find the word "epigram" used exactly. How far must we yield to Elizabethan usage?

I am inclined to think that the problems facing us are not so difficult as they may appear, or as they have sometimes been represented. For a beginning let us accept the definition of "epigram" given in the *New English Dictionary*: "A short poem ending in a witty or ingenious turn of thought, to which the rest of the composition is intended to lead up." I do not say this will cover all the compositions termed "epigrams" by early writers; yet it exactly fits a gratifyingly large proportion of them. Of course we must interpret with charity the words "witty or ingenious turn," sometimes taking the will for the deed. In general it may be said (as later it will be shown) that the difficulty of deciding whether a poem is an epigram or merely epigrammatic is no greater than that experienced in distinguishing between the formal satire and the satirical or the humorous; while it is rather less than the difficulty of separating the true lyric from other kinds of poetry classed as lyrical.

We can test our definition in a concrete manner. Here are four epigrams by as many writers, representing four different uses of this poetical species. The first, taken from *The Letting of Humours Blood in the Head Vaine* (1600) by Samuel Rowlands, represents what we might call generalized satire. It is on the very common subject of woman:

> Wee men, in many faultes abound,
> But two, in women can be found:
> The worst that from their sex proceedes,
> Is naught in wordes, and naught in deedes.

The next is taken from *The Scourge of Folly* (1611) by John Davies of Hereford. It represents the great class of epigrams which seem to be directed at particular persons,

but which conceal the identities of those persons by the use
of classical names:

OF CLOPHUS HIS HELPES IN ARGUING

Clophus hath two great helpes in reasoning,
Although his reasons neuer help his sense;
Yet he in disputation still is king
Through brutish ignorance and impudence:
   Put by your helpes and with you Ile dispute,
   If not, I yeelde more reason being mute.

The third is a sepulchral epigram, Ben Jonson's "On Sir
John Roe"; such a poem was intended, as the first couplet
indicates, to be pinned upon the bier of the deceased:

In place of scutcheons that should deck thy hearse,
   Take better ornaments, my tears and verse.
If any sword could save from Fates', Roe's could;
   If any Muse outlive their spight, his can:
If any friends' tears could restore, his would;
   If any pious life ere lifted man
To heaven; his hath: O happy state! wherein
   We, sad for him, may glory, and not sin.

The fourth represents the adulatory or complimentary epigram, addressed to the living; sometimes, as here, by one
author to another. It is taken from John Weever's *Epigrammes in the Oldest Cut and the Newest Fashion* (1599):

AD IO: MARSTON, ET BEN: IOHNSON

Marston, thy Muse enharbours Horace vaine,
Then some Augustus giue thee Horace merit,
And thine, embuskin'd Iohnson, doth retaine
So rich a stile, and wondrous gallant spirit;
That if to praise your Muses I desired,
My Muse would muse. Such wittes must be admired.

These four specimens cannot be said to represent the whole various volume of epigram-writing; but they have been picked almost at random, and are typical of thousands more. Cannot it be said of each that it is "a short poem ending in a witty or ingenious turn of thought, to which the rest of the composition is intended to lead up"? Antithesis, paradox, and punning provide the witty and ingenious turns. Ben Jonson's tribute to his friend, for example, employs antithesis in the point, but that point rests mainly upon paradox—the double paradox of being sad yet glorying, of glorying and yet not sinning. Antithesis, we shall find, is the stock figure of the epigrammatic point. Can antithesis be called a manifestation of ingenuity or wit? Not always a manifestation, surely, but a very proper accompaniment. Furthermore, to cast one's thought into antithetic form is likely to heighten concision and sententiousness.

This train of thought leads me to suggest a slight amendment to our definition, one based upon the rhetorical teaching of the sixteenth century, and the resultant practice. We know what stress that century placed upon sententiousness—or "sentence," as it was sometimes called. If we are to give epigrammatists of the time their due, we should amend our definition by inserting the words, "or sententious comment," after "witty or ingenious turn." For the point of an epigram—and I believe this holds true for the Classical period as well as for the Renaissance—does not always depend upon a *turn* of thought: the thought may go straight forward, and the point may be merely an emphatic summary of what has already been presented, or a distillation from it. The figure of *epiphonema* or *acclamatio* (the same thing under Greek and Latin names) was taught in the schools as a part of the resources of an epigrammatist. Epiphonema is defined in the *New English Dictionary* as "an exclamatory sentence or striking reflection which sums up or concludes a discourse or a passage in the discourse." The suitability of this figure to the point of an epigram was mentioned by Erasmus in his *Copia Verborum*:[2]

"... Now another kind of *sententia* [striking sentiment], called *epiphonema* by the Greeks, Quintilian calls *acclamatio*. It is the final acclamation of [*i.e.*, the cry of assent to or approval of] the thing narrated or proved. ... This kind is suited to epigrams; as in the epigram about the ewe which nourished a wolf's whelp at its dugs: 'Nature is never subverted in its functions.'[3] Likewise in Martial a poem often is concluded with a verse of *epiphonema*: as, 'Either keep awake or dream about yourself, Nasidienus,' and, 'Do you want to know what you are? You are a great dabbler.'" And in *The Arte of English Poesie* (1589), which offers an excellent summary of the more superficial parts of rhetoric as then taught, Erasmus's hint to epigrammatists is repeated:[4]

"Our poet in his short ditties, but specially playing the Epigrammatist, will vse to conclude and shut up his Epigram with a verse or two, spoken in such sort, as it may seeme a manner of allowance to all the premisses, and that with a ioyfull approbation, which the Latines call *Acclamatio*. ... Sir Philip Sidney very pretily closed vp a dittie in this sort.

What medicine then, can such disease remoue,

Where loue breedes hate, and hate engenders loue."[5]

---

[2] Liber II, *De sententiis*; here translated.

[3] The epigram referred to is in the Greek Anthology, Paton's edition (Loeb Classical Library), III, p. 26, 27. Erasmus quoted the epigram in full, and translated it into Latin, in his *Adagia* (*Opera Omnia*, II, 442); and Timothe Kendall printed two English versions made from Erasmus's Latin, in *Flowers of Epigrammes* (1577).

The epigrams of Martial quoted from in the next sentence are VII, 54, and II, 7.

[4] Arber's reprint (1869), p. 225.

[5] This example is not the best for the point I have been making, for Sidney's *acclamatio* displays antithesis and paradox as well as sententiousness. I do not wish to say that *acclamatio* never involved a turn of thought;

Recalling the primitive relation of the epigram to the inscription, we see the propriety of allowing a "sentence" to stand as the point of an epigram, even if it does not involve wit or ingenuity. There is a kind of ingenuity, of course, in complete conciseness; and compression frequently results in paradox.

It may be objected that in all this we have in mind only the Martialian or Roman epigram, and are forgetting the Greek. The distinction is indeed important enough to be kept alive; let us introduce it by means of an anecdote set down in *Menagiana*:

". . . M. de Racan one day went to see Mademoiselle de Gournay, who showed him some epigrams she had written and asked his opinion of them. M. de Racan did not care for them, and said that they lacked point. 'That does not matter at all,' said Mademoiselle de Gournay, 'for these are epigrams *a la Grecque*.' Afterwards, they went together to dine at the house of M. de Lorme. Their host having set before them a *potage* which was not very good, Mademoiselle de Gournay turned to M. de Racan and said: 'What a vile soup!' 'Mademoiselle,' replied he, 'it is a soup *a la Grecque*.' This phrase was repeated so widely that in many circles 'soup *a la Grecque*' became the usual designation for a tasteless *potage*; and one said of a poor cook, 'He makes soup *a la Grecque*.' "[6]

"The true or best form of the early Greek epigram does not aim at wit or seek to produce surprise," wrote Lord

I am emphasizing only that a satisfactory point, using the figure of *acclamatio*, could be made without a turn.

A bit of monologue supposed to have come from Scotland illustrates this last statement: "Ah, Duncan, ye should ha' been wi' us at Tammas Cartwright's hoose on the Sabbath morn. There was Tammas himsel' and mesel' and Robert MacGregor and Sandy Speirs in Tammas's back parlor, and each man wi' his pipes and each playin' a tune to his own mind. Mon, it was juist heaven!"

[6] (Amsterdam, 1716), I, 138. Here freely translated.

Neaves. "Its purpose is to set forth in the shortest, simplest, and plainest language, but yet with perfect purity and even elegance of diction, some fact or feeling of such interest as would prompt the real or supposed speaker to record it in the form of an epigram."[7] J. W. Mackail, who has led many modern readers to an understanding delight in the Anthology, defines the Greek epigram as "in its first intention . . . a very short poem summing up as though in a memorial inscription what it is desired to make permanently memorable in a single action or situation."[8] We should notice at once that these writers are laying stress upon the early Greek epigram, and that within the Anthology itself the change to the Martialian type takes place. Professor Mackail himself says that by Martial's time the Greek epigrammatists were writing like Martial. Hence only a rather small share of the Greek Anthology is really written *a la Grecque*. Some late Greek writers—and Roman and English writers—wrote in the early Greek manner; on the other hand, there are epigrams written as early as the time of Plato which lead up to a point or an antithetical turn of thought.[9]

Nor were the Greek poets in any period entirely heedless of the opportunity offered in the conclusion of an epigram. J. A. Symonds has written: "The Greek epigram has this, in fact, in common with all good poems, that the conclusion should be the strongest and most emphatic portion."[10] It is true that Martial turned a greater share of attention to the "ingenious or witty turn" at the end, with the result that

[7] In his Introduction to *The Greek Anthology*, Blackwood edition (1874).

[8] *Select Epigrams from the Greek Anthology* (revised edition, 1906), p. 4.

[9] For example, *Anthologia Palatina*, xi, 235, by Demodocus, who is quoted by Aristotle: "The Chians are bad, not one bad and another not, but all bad except Procles,—and Procles is a Chian." (Paton's translation.) Another example is the celebrated quatrain, attributed to Plato, of the aged Lais offering her mirror to Venus.

[10] *Studies of the Greek Poets* (New York, 1879), ii, 332.

the sting or point has come to be of the essence. But Professor Mackail certainly overstates when he says: "The chance of language has restricted the word in its modern use to a sense which it never bore in Greek at all, defined in the line of Boileau, *un bon mot de deux rimes orné*."[11] For Boileau did not so define the epigram; he said that in his time epigrams *often* were no more than that, implying that *usually* they were, as they should be, something else.

Of the Greek epigram, then, I should say first that in its primitive type (the type which is contrasted with the Martialian) it represents a form close to the simple inscription which is the origin of all epigram-writing. Yet that fact alone does not account wholly for its difference from the later epigram.[12] This difference is accounted for rather by changes in rhetorical taste and practice from age to age. What seemed to one generation to be the perfect comment would have struck readers of a later generation as flat and frigid. Martial, a Spaniard by birth, was more fertile in rhetorical resources, more ingenious and less restrained in their use, than his predecessors had been. Yet this difference is not an essential one. Readers in all ages want the perfect comment—but what seems perfect differs as times change. In the second place, let it be noted that the quality in the Greek Anthology which commentators love to emphasize, the element of sincere, passionate, yet restrained statement, is a lyrical rather than an epigrammatical quality; and is to be sought for, in later periods, in lyrics rather than in epigrams. The concept of "pure lyricism" is a fairly modern one. Within it we have encompassed much that the ancients and even men of the Renaissance would have been willing to allow to the epigram. To put the matter bluntly,

[11] *Op. cit.*, p. 5.
[12] It is quite possible to use "pointed" lines as a "practical" inscription: see, for instances, Gay's epitaph upon himself and Pope's inscription for the collar of the Prince of Wales' dog.

the moment an epigram becomes very good—if it is not too funny or too obviously ingenious—it is now in danger of being classed as a lyric. Landor's "Rose Aylmer" is a case in point. And for this reason, our modern definition of the epigram, even with the amendment I have suggested, cannot be an infallible touchstone for testing the productions of past ages.

Yet everything here said supports the conclusion that epigram-literature, instead of having suffered a cleavage at the time of Martial, is fairly unified, and clearly continuous, from its beginnings in the inscription down to its modern development in prose.[13] This trend of thought is strengthened, and additional light is thrown upon the epigram, when we turn to Lessing, whose *Anmerkungen über das Epigramm*[14] is a mine of good things. Writing with much classical literature in mind, with the treatises of Vavasseur, Batteux, Scaliger, and others before him (not to mention the three thousand epigrams of Logau, those of Warnecke, and his own), Lessing sets down this interesting definition: "The epigram is a poem in which, after the manner of an inscription proper, our attention and curiosity are aroused with reference to some one particular object, and more or less held in suspense, in order to be gratified at a single stroke."

He had attacked his problem by asking, What is the relation of the modern or literary epigram to its original—the inscription? His answer, in part, follows:

"The true inscription is not to be thought of apart from that whereon it stands, or might stand. Both together make

---

[13] This last stage in its history I treat of briefly in Chapter XVII. [Never written—eds.]

[14] *Zerstreute Anmerkungen über das Epigramm, und einige der vornehmsten Epigrammatisten*, first published as a part of *Vermischte Schriften* (Berlin, 1771). It was translated into English by J. and H. L. Hunt in the volume, *Fables and Epigrams: with Essays on Fable and Epigram* (1825). The passages here translated in the text will be found in Lessing's *Sämtliche Schriften*, ed. Lachmann (Stuttgart, 1895), XI, 217.

the whole from which arises the impression which, speaking generally, we ascribe to the inscription alone. First, some object of sense which arouses our curiosity; and then the account of this same object, which satisfies that curiosity.

"But who is there that can run over in his mind either a small or a great stock of epigrams, to whom it does not immediately occur that, similarly, two parts can be distinguished in almost every one of them? And certainly most clearly in those which will strike him as coming nearest to the perfect epigram. They all divide naturally into two parts, in one of which our attention is called to some specific object, our curiosity awakened about some particular subject; while in the second our attention reaches its mark, our curiosity finds an explanation."

The first of these two parts of the epigram Lessing called the "expectation" or the "anticipation" (*Erwartung*); the second part is the "disclosure" or "explanation" (*Aufschluss*).[15] Thus in the following epigram (from William Goddard's *Neaste of Waspes*, 1615),

> A Judge t'a surgeon came: Surgeon, quoth hee,
> My arme is sore, what ist soe payneth mee?
> The surgeon looking on it, sir, hee cryes,

[15] In a very good summary of Lessing's ideas a writer in the *North British Review*, LXII (1865), 42-64, uses the terms "preparation" and "point." T. K. Whipple, in *Martial and the English Epigram from Sir Thomas Wyatt to Ben Jonson* (Berkeley, 1925), uses "exposition" and "conclusion."

Other pairs of terms, used by commentators writing in Latin, are: *expositio* and *clausula*, *indicatio* and *conclusio*, *protasis* and *apodosis*, *subjectum* and *proedicatum*. J. C. Brandelius, from whose *Dissertatio Theoriam Epigrammatis Percensens* (Upsala, 1810) the foregoing list is taken, himself uses *expectatio* and *solutio*. J. G. Herder used *Darstellung* (presentation) and *Befriedigung* (satisfaction), as being better suited to his own theory than were Lessing's terms.

We should note that the two parts of the epigram had been distinguished by writers earlier than Lessing; his contribution was to point out the analogy with an object (a statue, for example) and its inscription.

Oh much corruption in your arme there lies.
A poore man by, cryes, Surgeon understand,
'Tis not in's arme, corrupted is his hand,

the first four lines present the situation, or, as Lessing
would say, direct the attention to a certain object. We can
hardly say that they arouse the curiosity; for there is
nothing unusual in hearing that a judge was told by a
surgeon that his sore arm had corruption in it. Still, the
reader will be, at worst, in the state of mind represented by
the question, "What of it?" The last two lines, the disclosure, answer this question: they justify the calling of
attention to the situation.

Lessing himself was aware that the first part of the epigram, the *Erwartung*, frequently is taken care of by the
title, or, as in many of the Greek epigrams, lies outside of
what is set down and must be assumed. In such instances
the epigram is all *Aufschluss*. The title, then, or the supplied subject, takes the place of the statue or building for
which an inscription is to be written; the epigram is the
inscription.[16] Hence we occasionally find an epigram with
a title (technically speaking, *lemma*) longer than itself. Such
is the tribute of Utenhove, a Dutch writer, to the learned
Scotchman, George Buchanan:

IN I SANNA. H FRANCAST. A FLAM. H VID. A NAUGER.

P BEMB. ITALOS: MICH HOSP. ADR. TORNEB.

IO AURAT. GALLOS: & GEORG. BUCHAN.

SCOTUM

Tres Italos Galli senos vicere, sed vnum
Vincere Scotigenam non valuere nouem.

[16] Here is an important bond between the verse-epigram and the prose
epigrams which we now find in plays and essays. In these, the *Erwartung*
is supplied by the circumstances or by the preceding material. As I show
in a later chapter, before 1650 the epigram had begun to be thought of as
a point only, apart from the preparation for it.

Three Frenchmen did Italians six
for learnyng great excell:
But from them all one Scot alone
doth beare away the bell.[17]

Robert Hayman, in *Quodlibets* (1628), once put part of the preparation or exposition in prose:

What have Foolish men to doe with Princes Secrets?
Thought upon, on the preparation of a great Fleet, and may serve for all such actions hereafter.

Fond men doe wonder where this Fleet shall goe:
I should more wonder, if that I should know.

The chief difficulty in applying Lessing's definition arises in connection with his phrase, "some one particular object." How specific, how occasional, must the subject of the epigram be? If too general and abstract, does not the epigram become an apothegm or a maxim? Thus Lessing censures Batteux for allowing these verses by Pelisson to stand as an epigram:

Grandeur, savoir, renommée,
Amitié, plaisir, et bien,
Tout n'est que vent, que fumée:
Pour mieux dire, tout n'est rien.

This may be an interesting thought, he says, "but where is the occasion of this thought? Where is the specific peculiar circumstance—for such must be the occasion—through which the poet has arrived at this thought, and by which he leads the reader to it?" If this test were applied strictly, it might rule out of epigram-literature Sir John Harington's famous couplet on treason (*Epigrams*, 1618):

Treason doth never prosper: what's the reason?
Why if it prosper, none dare call it treason.

---

[17] From the address "To the reader" in Kendall's *Flowers of Epigrammes*, 1577. The translation is Kendall's own.

Here is some attempt, however, at creating an occasion. The first line constitutes an *Erwartung*, wherein the author calls our attention to the subject of treason and attempts to arouse our curiosity about it. But the subject is general rather than particular, and Lessing might object to calling the couplet an epigram.[18]

At least we must grant the validity of his distinction between an epigram and a maxim. "The typical satirical epigram," says Tucker, "must be not only comparatively short, but *complete*; not only witty, but *concrete*; not general, but *specific, occasional*."[19] Tucker is describing "the typical satirical epigram," the most epigrammatic of epigrams. Taking that as a norm, we might say that other varieties grade down from it: on one side in the direction of the maxim, proverb, or gnomic verse (as in those we have just considered); on another side in the direction of the lyric (as in some Greek epigrams and in epigrammatic madrigals and songs); on another side in the direction of the satirical essay (as in character-epigrams and those directed against vices); on another side in the direction of the verse-epistle or the elegy (as in commendatory verses); while in epitaphs and funereal epigrams the tendency is toward the dirge or threnody. As we proceed we shall have occasion to illustrate all of these tendencies.

The lore of the epigram, as the sixteenth century knew it, was summed up by Julius Caesar Scaliger in his *Poetices libri septem* (1561). Like Lessing, Scaliger practiced the art he treated of; but he did not so clearly perceive its nature, and in spite of his dictum, *non enim decuit argutissimi poematis praecepta sine argutia tradere*, his chapter on epigrams with its *Appendix pro Epigrammate*, is likely to

---

[18] The proverb-epigram, of which Harington's is an example, is discussed at some length *infra*, in connection with the work of John Heywood.

[19] *Verse-Satire in England Before the Renaissance* (New York, 1908), p. 17.

prove disappointing to a modern reader. His definition has only the virtue of being inclusive: "An epigram, therefore, is a short poem with a simple rating (*indicatione*) of some thing or other, some person or other, some fact or other; or deducing something from propositions."[20] By way of classifying epigrams Scaliger first tries to fit them into the Aristotelian division of speeches—judicial, suasory (deliberative), and demonstrative—citing Catullus's "Let us live, my Lesbia, and let us love," as an example of the suasory kind! In his *Appendix*, however, he makes another classification, one which was frequently cited by his successors and which, while not cutting very deep, is at least based on wide and discerning observation. He finds three main classes—the gentle, or easy-going, the lively, or pointed, and the multiplex, or composite. The first class includes amatory and adulatory epigrams, as exemplified by those of Catullus; to these he applies the term *mel*, or honey. The second class he subdivides into four varieties. First, there are foul and obscene epigrams, whose authors should be excluded not only from Plato's republic but also from the whole world. Second, there are those characterized by *fel*, or gall; these are the very bitter, the objurgatory and disparaging, "which, however, it is permitted to a good man to employ." To the third variety he applies the term *acetum*, or vinegar; "this mordant kind castigates without insult." Fourth, there are epigrams characterized by *sal*, or salt; "from these a laugh is got without that vituperation, and indeed with very little mordancy." By including a third main class, the multiplex, Scaliger contradicts the word *simplici* in his definition. Now he allows that an epigram may contain more than one point, may, indeed, consist of a series of distichs, each making a point. As is obvious, this development of the epigram (which can be illustrated in the English works of our

---

[20] The last phrase seems to have been added for the sake of epigrams based upon proverbs; see the discussion of this variety, *infra*, pp. 148-151.

period) relates it to the satirical essay and to other varieties of didactic poetry.

From 1589 forward, English readers could turn to the discussion of epigrams in the anonymous *Arte of English Poesie*, under the heading (Book I, Chapter xxvii), "The manner of Poesie by which they vttered their bitter taunts, and priuy nips, or witty scoffes and other merry conceits." By way of definition the author writes: "For this *Epigramme* is but an inscription or writing made as it were vpon a table, or in a windowe, or vpon the wall or mantell of a chimney in some place of common resort, where it was allowed euery man might come, or be sitting to chat and prate, as now in our tauernes and common tabling houses, where many merry heades meete, and scrible with ynke, with chalke, or with a cole such matters as they would euery man should know, and descant vpon. Afterward the same came to be put in paper and in bookes, and vsed as ordinarie missiues, some of friendship, some of defiaunce, or as other messages of mirth." Beyond this, there is little here concerning the theory of the epigram; though the author in other chapters quotes epigrams (sometimes his own) and offers advice to the epigrammatist. The chapter following the one already cited deals with epitaphs, and begins: "An Epitaph is but a kind of Epigram only applied to the report of the dead persons estate and degree, or of his other good or bad partes, to his commendation or reproch: and is an inscription such as a man may commodiously write or engraue vpon a tombe in few verses, pithie, quicke and sententious for the passer to peruse, and iudge vpon without any long tariaunce: So as if it exceede the measure of an Epigram, it is then (if the verse be correspondent) rather an Elegie then an Epitaph." The remainder of the chapter enforces the warning against overlong epitaphs. Passing to the next chapter but one, we find the heading, "Of short Epigrames called Posies." This treats of the monostichs or distichs which might be sent as

New Year's gifts, inscribed in dishes of marchpane, painted upon trenchers, or engraved upon rings. Except for listing these uses, nothing is said of the posy.

Among other difficulties of classification, as has been suggested before, is that of distinguishing the epigram, in certain of its manifestations, from the lyric. Professor F. E. Schelling, in an early chapter of his work, *The English Lyric* (1913), treats of this difficulty with great penetration. After attempting to disentangle the lyric from other affiliated poetical species, very much as we have been attempting to disentangle the epigram, he writes:

"In conclusion of these matters, be it remarked that in anthologies of English poetry the epigram has sometimes trespassed on the domain of the lyric. The epigram is often musical and commonly short, and here the resemblance between it and the lyric ends. For the epigram is intellectual, rhetorical, and conscious, addressed to stir in the hearer an approval of art; the lyric is emotional, poetic, and unconscious, in so far as a piece of artistry often involving a loving elaboration may exist for its own end and only secondarily for the pleasure which it is its legitimate function to occasion in the hearer or reader."

There was much confusion—indeed, virtual identification —of rhetoric and poetry in the period of the Renaissance, as there has also been later. "My greatest approbation," wrote Erasmus, "is reserved for a rhetorical poem and poetical oratory. . . the rhetorical art should transpire through the poem."[21] This idea is strong in literary theory and practice for many years both before and after Erasmus wrote. Considering rhetoric as discourse which is designed primarily for the sake of an effect (either as display or as persuasion) upon a certain audience, and poetry, in its pure state, as "the

[21] In a letter; translated by Woodward, *Desiderius Erasmus Concerning the Aim and Method of Education* (Cambridge, 1904), p. 124.

spontaneous overflow of powerful feelings," we see that the rhetorical impulse colored most of the literature of the period we wish to consider. Even lyrics, as Professor Schelling would agree, did not escape this coloring; and at best he can be sure of distinguishing only the predominantly poetical from the obviously rhetorical. But he is right when he puts epigrams in the realm of rhetoric. "Eloquence is written to be heard, poetry to be overheard," is Mill's famous apothegm. Epigrams are always written to be heard. Their authors address them to an audience. They have the touch of epideictic rhetoric, the touch of display; and they frequently have as well the persuasive purpose. This last is stated epigrammatically by Robert Hayman in his *Quodlibets* (1628):

TO THE READER

Sermons and epigrams have a like end,
To improve, to reprove, and to amend.
Some passe without this use, 'cause they are witty;
And so doe many Sermons, more's the pitty.

As a matter of fact, the distinction between the song and the epigram formed the subject of considerable discussion in the eighteenth century.[22] The editor of *The Festoon*,[23] a popular anthology of epigrams, though using different terms, expresses ideas very similar to those of the foregoing paragraph. He writes:

"An Essay upon song-writing, published in the Guardian, makes the whole difference between a Song and an Epigram to consist in the subject only: That an epigram is

[22] See, for example, the "Critical Dissertation" prefixed to *A Collection of Epigrams* (London, 1735), thought by some to be the work of William Oldys.

[23] Second edition, London, 1767. The editor was Rev. Richard Graves, M.A. His introductory essay also appears in *The Christmas Treat* (Dublin, 1767).

usually employed upon satyrical occasions; and that the business of the song is chiefly to express

> *'Love's pleasing cares, and the free joys of wine.'*

But, if I might venture to differ from so distinguished a writer, I should rather say, That, whatever the subject be, *tenderness of sentiment* and an impassioned expression are essential to a song; as the usually narrative style of an epigram seems incompatible with the soft raptures of music. How ridiculous must it be to hear a Frenchman quavering out

> *'Tu parles mal par tout de moy*
> *Je dis du bien par tout de toy.'*
>
> *'Thou speakest always ill of me,*
> *I speak always well of thee.'*

Which translation of an epigram from Buchanan,[24] was a favourite song in France: As, on the contrary, the tender sentiments and plaintive style of a lover appear inconsistent with the studied turns of an epigram—for

> *'Who can chuse but pitty*
> *A dying swain so miserably witty?'* "

Questions concerning the length of an epigram also have stirred up controversy. Jean Vauquelin, a French poet and epigrammatist of our period, expressed the common sense of most readers and writers in his quatrain "De L'Epigramme":

> Mon grand Duc, une belle ame
> Tousiours court fait l'Epigramme;
> Car qui trop long le feront
> Un Poeme ce feroit.

Some free souls among the writers, however, from Martial down, have protested that they should judge for themselves

---

[24] Imitated from the Greek.

what length is allowable; so that the business of the student seems to be merely to count the lines. J. W. Mackail's report upon the Greek Anthology, that the epigrams therein vary from two to twenty-eight lines in length but rarely exceed twelve, may be taken as generally true for all epigram-literature. Martial at least once allows himself to run to forty-two lines; but his usual practice conforms to the statement made above. His retort to a critic who charged him with writing epigrams too long has been translated thus:

"Cosconius, who think my epigrams long, you would be useful for greasing axles. On this principle you would fancy the Colossus to be tall, and would describe Brutus' boy as short. Learn what you are ignorant of: often two pages of Marsus and of learned Pedo treat of a single theme. Things are not long from which you can subtract nothing; but you, Cosconius, make your distichs long."[25]

We may say at once that by far the greater part of epigrams in English are in six lines or fewer, with couplets and quatrains predominating. Yet it is not strange that writers should refuse to be confined to these lengths, and say with Thomas Bancroft (*Two Books of Epigrams*, 1632):

Though Epigrams be but a curter kind
Of satyrs, striking on as sharpe a string,
To dysticks or tetrasticks do not bind
My free-borne Muse, for youth would have its swing.

Let us end this chapter with a word about the subjects of epigrams. Our definitions have suggested no limitation to the possible subjects; nor is there such a limitation in practice. *Epigrammatum autem genera tot sunt, quot rerum,* wrote Scaliger; "for there are as many kinds of epigrams as of things." He goes on: "They are expressed in as many kinds of verses as there are. They are composed in as many

---

[25] By Walter C. A. Ker in *Martial*, Loeb Classical Library. The epigram is II, 77.

words and kinds of words, forms, shapes, figures, and modes as there are kinds, species, forms, figures, and sorts of words in the entire range of languages, nations, peoples, and races." Let one of our English epigrammatists speak for himself. Thomas Bastard opens his *Chrestoleros* (1598) with the following poem, which Robert Herrick found worthy of imitation when he wrote the introductory verses for his *Hesperides*, fifty years later:

> I speake of wants, of frauds, of policies,
> Of manners, and of vertues and of times,
> Of vnthrifts and of friends, and enemies,
> Poets, Physitions, Lawyers, and Diuines,
> Of vsurers, buyers, borrowers, ritch and poore,
> Of theeues, and murtherers, by sea and land,
> Of pickthankes, lyers, flatterers lesse and more,
> Of good and bad, and all that comes to hand;
> I speake of hidden and of open things:
> Of strange euents, of countries farre and wide,
> Of warres, of captaynes, Nobles, Princes, kings,
> *Asia, Europe,* and all the world beside.
>   This is my subiect, reader, I confesse,
>   From which I thinke seldom I doe digresse.

And yet, by reason of the force of classical tradition, within this limitless range of subject-matter, certain themes persistently recur, almost *ad nauseam*. Some of these are named in the following passage, written to describe the epigram in Italian literature; such was the strength of classical example, however, that the description applies perfectly to English epigram-writing:

"Exclusively moral, the satire seems to know only how to chastise the proverbial loquacity of woman or the sly greediness of the monk; the miser who drowns himself to save the halter; the physician whose victims enlarge the bounds of the cemetery; the faithless wife; the aged coquette whose hair, teeth, and heart are all artificial; the old libertine, etc. Some epigrams are only sayings or aphorisms, some resemble the madrigal, or appear versions of anecdotes, stories, or *contes*; others, finally, are rather apologues or caustic epitaphs. How many of these modern witticisms are nothing but variations of the oldest themes, and how often one theme, like certain notes, is repeated to satiety!"[26]

The matters discussed in this chapter receive abundant illustration as we proceed. For treatment of such other topics as might belong here, let me refer the reader to M. Colletet, with his chapters "De la pointe de l'Epigramme," "Comme on peut discerner une bonne Epigramme d'avec une mauvaise," and so on, or to other of the numerous writers upon the craft and mystery of the epigrammatist.[27]

[26] G. Setti, "L'Epigramma italiano e l'ultimo degli Epigrammisti," *Nuova Antologia*, cvii (1889), 627-655. The passage I quote is as translated by T. F. Crane in *The Romanic Review*, xi (1920), 275.

[27] Besides the essays of Scaliger, Colletet, Lessing, and Brandelius, referred to in text or notes, one has at one's disposal: Thom. Correas, *De toto eo poematis genere quod epigramma vulgo dicitur* (Venice, 1569); Jo. Cottunius, *De conficiendo Epigrammate* (Bonn, 1632); Nicholas Mercier, *De conscribendo epigrammate* (Paris, 1653); François Vavasseur, *De Epigrammate liber* (Paris, 1669); Charles Batteux, "Traité de l'Epigramme et de l'Inscription," in *Principes de la Litterature* (Paris, 1774).

J. G. Herder criticized Lessing's views upon the epigram, in his "Anmerkung über das griechische Epigramm," *Sammtliche Werke* (Berlin, 1888), xv, 337 ff.; and J. G. Sulzer carried on the discussion in his *Allgemeine Theorie der Schönen Kunste* (2d ed.; Leipzig, 1794), iv, 393 ff.

Τὸ πρῶτον Μῶρος, τὸ δὲ δεύτερον εἷλεν Ἔρασμος,
Τὸ τρίτον ἐκ Μουσῶν στέμμα Μίκυλλος ἔχει.

—DR. SAMUEL JOHNSON[1]

CHAPTER II · THE EPIGRAMS OF
SIR THOMAS MORE

WE may begin with a story, probably untrue, which is told by Thomas Fuller. On a certain occasion while William Grocyn, later to become a pioneer of Greek studies in England, was attending Winchester School, a girl threw a snowball at him. Young Grocyn commemorated the attack and its consequences in these verses:

> Me nive candenti petiit mea Julia: rebar
> Igne carere nivem, nix tamen ignis erat.
> Sola potes nostras extinguere Julia flammas,
> Non nive, non glacie, sed potes igne pari.

Fuller translates:

> A snow-ball white at me did Julia throw:
> Who would suppose it? fire was in that snow.
> Julia alone can quench my hot desire,
> But not with snow, or ice, but equal fire.[2]

---

[1] In his diary, July 15, 1774. Croker (his edition of Boswell's *Life*, 1831, III, 127) translates: "More bore away the first crown of the Muses, Erasmus the second, and Micyllus has the third." Jacob Micyllus, born Moltzer (1503-1558), was a German scholar and Neo-Latin poet.

[2] *Worthies of England*, ed. Nuttall (1840), III, 118. Fuller, though following Pits and Bale, felt doubtful about the attribution to Grocyn, and noted: "These verses are printed among Petronius's Fragments, being a farrago of many verses later than that ancient author." They comprise the first and last distichs of an eight-line poem doubtfully ascribed to Petronius Arbiter; see *Poetae Latinae Minores*, ed. Baehrens (Leipzig, 1882), IV, 101. A sixteenth-century translation, by Sir Nicholas Bacon, will be found in *The Recreations of His Age* (Oxford, 1903; issued 1919), p. 35.

The poem somehow became connected with that shadowy poet Afranius,

The incident illustrates the fashion of verse-writing as it was carried on among schoolboys and scholars of the Renaissance. Not always, to be sure, were the occasions of writing so slight and so personal as here; not always were the poems so short.

The voluminous collection of *poemata* gathered by the tireless Jean Gruter and published at Frankfort in 1612 contains nearly 250,000 pieces, the work of German writers alone.[3] Scholars, nobles, kings, bishops, cardinals, and popes vied with one another in producing Latin verse. Says Marsden, in *Philomorus*:

". . . Latin verses were poured out in copious streams and in every form of composition—elegy, ode, epistle, and even epic poem. They were written upon every conceivable subject, whether sacred or secular. In the intellectual banquet

or Petronius Afranius (cf. Collignon, *Étude sur Pétrone* [Paris, 1892], p. 281; Teuffel, *A History of Roman Literature*, trans. by Wagner, 1873, II, 89), and Christopher Smart's English translation of it appears in Chalmers's *English Poets* (XVI, 58) as "From the Latin of Petronius *Ascanius*"! I have not learned whether Smart or Chalmers introduced this new ghost. The Latin poem, ascribed to "Incognitus," with an English translation by Robert Vilvain, will be found in that author's *Enchiridium Epigrammatum* (1654); and again, ascribed to Petronius Afranius, with a new translation and an interesting editorial note, in the *Works* (2d ed., 1793, I, 162) of Soames Jenyns. Finally, let me say that the eight-line poem is reprinted in an unimportant anthology, *Carmina Praestantium Poetarum* . . . Io. Antonii Taygeti . . . selecta (Brescia, 1565), as the work of Marcus Antonius Flaminius (1498-1550)! These facts will suggest the difficulties sometimes encountered in tracing the authorship of an epigram.

[3] *Delitiae Poetarum Germanorum*, in six volumes (the editor's name is concealed under the initials A. F. G. G.); I have not counted the poems but accept the figure from Marsden's *Philomorus*. There were also, collected by Gruter, *Delitiae Poetarum Italorum*, two vols., n. p. [Frankfort], 1608; *Delitiae Poetarum Gallorum*, three vols., n. p. [Frankfort], 1609; and *Delitiae Poetarum Belgicorum*, three vols., Frankfort, 1614. For all three of these collections he used the pseudonym Ranutius Gherus. *Delitiae Poetarum Hungarorum*, four vols., edited by Johannes Philippus Pareus, appeared at Frankfort in 1619; *Delitiae Poetarum Scotorum*, edited by Arthur Johnston, at Amsterdam in 1637; and *Delitiae Poetarum Danorum*, edited by Friderich Rostgaard, two vols., at Leyden in 1693.

thus provided, the solid and substantial dishes were followed by the more piquant Epigrammata."[4]

In another place, Marsden writes concerning these *epigrammata*:

". . . Whether eulogy was intended or satire, they were equally available. A writer could flatter the more adroitly and also satirize the more bitingly than if he used the vernacular language of the country. Sannazarius wrote six lines in praise of the city of Venice, for which he was rewarded with an honorarium of 600 golden crowns. Ulrich von Hutten consoled himself under the troubles of life by attacking his personal enemies, and by writing during the war vigorous Epigrammata against Venice and Pope Julius II."[5]

We cannot here pursue the whole subject of Latin poetry in the Renaissance;[6] but it is necessary that we notice the classification of poems which became prevalent, and understand the nomenclature generally used. In reading the title pages of Neo-Latin collections, we notice that *poemata* is the general term most frequently used to include all varieties, though *carmina* sometimes does this service. Specifically, however, *carmen* denotes a song. Other specific terms which are readily understood are *odae, epigrammata, epitaphia, epithalamia, hymni, eclogae, encomia, epistolae*, and *elegiae*. Concerning this last term it may be repeated that

---

[4] p. 22. This pleasant study of Sir Thomas More's Latin poetry was published anonymously in 1842 and again, enlarged three-fold, in 1878. My citations are from the second edition. *Philomorus* has contributed much to my account of More's epigrams, but I am able frequently to supplement and occasionally to correct Marsden.

[5] pp. 6-7.

[6] For a good brief summary see Walter MacKellar, *The Latin Poems of John Milton* (Cornell Studies in English, 1930), pp. 4-14. For a more extended history, see F. A. Wright and T. A. Sinclair, *A History of Later Latin Literature* (1931). For French writers only, see D. Murarasu, *La Poésie Néo-Latine et la Renaissance des Lettres Antiques en France (1500-1549)* (Paris, 1928).

elegia did not denote a poem of grief—more often one of love—but meant rather a personal meditative poem. It will be recalled that Christopher Marlowe's translation of Ovid's *Amores* appeared under the title of *All Ovid's Elegies* (*c.* 1600). Explanations of other terms follow:

Amores—love poems, usually brief, after the model of Ovid's poems with that title or of the amatory poems of Catullus.

Emblemata—emblems; discussed *infra*, pp. 32-35.

Genethliaca—poems celebrating a birth; or birthday tributes to a friend or patron.

Icones—poems giving the *image* of a person; frequently written as inscriptions to be placed beneath pictures.

Naeniae—poems of mourning, dirges.

Querulae—complaints; corresponding to the various kinds of "complaints" found in English poetry.

Sylvae—"woods"; miscellaneous poems, similar to elegies, but sometimes satirical or familiar. "The word means literally 'pieces of raw material,' from *silva* Gr. ὑλη, *i.e.* pieces ready to be worked up into shape or impromptu pieces." (*Statius*, Loeb Classical Library, 1928, i, Intro., xi.) It should be noticed that the term began as a singular, collective one, meaning "timber," and that the use of *sylva* to mean a single poem, one of a collection of *sylvae*, came later. A fair history of the literary use of the word can be gleaned from Suetonius, *De Grammaticis*, x; Aulus Gellius, *Atticae Noctes*, preface vi; Quintilian, X, iii, 17. Ben Jonson illustrates the old use of ὑλη or *sylva* by his title *Timber*; the later, Neo-Latin uses are responsible for his *The Forest* and *Underwoods*.

It may be added that such general terms as *Juvenilia* and *Nugae* (trifles) frequently appear on title pages. Thus the epigram is not confined to the books or sections of *epigrammata*; but may appear among *epitaphia, encomia, genethliaca, emblemata, naeniae,* or *icones.*

It is against the European background here hinted at that we must view the Latin epigram-writing of Englishmen in the sixteenth and seventeenth centuries. Erasmus, who rightfully claims a place in any account of English Humanism, did his share of verse-making; small collections of *carmina* and *epigrammata* will be found as sections of his *Opera Omnia*.[7] His versification is correct and fairly easy, but some competent critics have judged that he lacked both poetic fire and poetic fancy. He felt some enthusiasm for the writing of poetry in his youth, but in his letters, which belong to his maturity, he always speaks slightingly or apologetically of his poems. As to epigram-writing, we may let Erasmus tell his own story: "There is no kind of composition," he says, "to which I have given less attention than to epigrams, though some of my epigrams were collected by partial friends and edited at Basel. To make the book more lively, they were joined with those of More, who is very happy in this kind of composition."[8]

The modesty of Erasmus in this regard seems justified; his epigrams have remained perhaps the least known and least influential of all his writings. His *Adagia*, his *Colloquia*, and his *Copia Verborum*, the first through containing suggestive materials for epigrammatists as well as some Latin versions of Greek epigrams, the others through their use as texts in rhetoric for many decades, had some influence upon epigram-writing;[9] but his own epigrams had no such influence. Timothe Kendall, our first anthologist of epigrams, included four translations from Erasmus in his *Flowers of Epigrammes* (1577); yet these are not from

---

[7] Le Clerc's edition (Leyden, 1703-06), I, 1215 ff.; v, 1318 ff.; and VIII, 561 ff. Some additions could be made from his letters: See Allen, *Erasmi Epistolae*, I, 473; II, 411; III, 124, 258. Preserved Smith in his *Erasmus* (New York, 1923) prints from manuscript two newly-discovered poems; one is a *Carmen extemporale* to John Skelton, which Professor Smith translates into English verse. Further important additions will be found in the Appendix of Albert Hyma's *The Youth of Erasmus* (Ann Arbor, 1930).

[8] In his "Catalogue of Lucubrations" at the end of *Compendium Vitae*; translation by F. M. Nichols, *The Epistles of Erasmus* (1901), I, 22.

[9] See *supra*, p. 5, for advice to the epigrammatist in *Copia Verborum*, and *infra*, pp. 148-149, for the pertinence of *Colloquia*. See also the following note.

poems originally by Erasmus, but are English versions of Greek epigrams quoted and translated (into Latin) in the *Adagia*.[10]

According to an account by Froben, many epigrams and other occasional verses were composed by Erasmus extempore, for those who begged them, sometimes interrupting his more serious labors. Erasmus himself says that some of his epigrams were composed while he was taking his walks or at wine with his friends. A few of his poems are to be found with their accompanying letters, in his collected *Epistolae*. One of these is especially interesting as proving that the greatest scholar of his age did not hold himself above writing acrostic verses requiring curious ingenuity. From the following letter and poem we see that Erasmus has written for a picture of Mary Magdalene an inscription which conceals (or reveals) the name of the Canon who was, perhaps, the donor of the picture:[11]

ERASMUS ROTERODAMUS TO JOHN MERLIBERCH OF DIEST, CANON OF THE COLLEGE OF THE BLESSED MARTIN, LOUVAIN:

The poem is trochaic tetrameter, catalectic. Take the first and last letters in each verse as far as the caesura (which is marked with a *virgula*) and then the first and last in the second part, and so on with all the rest, and you will have, as you wished, "Johannes Merliberch Diest."

IN LAVDEM DIVAE MARIAE MAGDALENAE

Impotenti amoris oestrO / Haec beata percitA
Nardicum profudit vngueN, / Eluit lacrymis pedeS,
Mox capillis tersit . eccE, / Rex Olympi, qui semeL
Illecebras spreuit ac suB- / Egit, istis ampliteR

---

10 In Kendall (Spenser Society, 1874), pp. 109-111; in Erasmus (Leyden ed.), II, 390, 503.

11 Allen, *Erasmi Epistolae*, IV, 323; the letter here translated. Allen dates it conjecturally in August, 1520.

Capitur oblectaculis . procH, / Daemonis technis malI
Eua capta est: ista lacrymiS / Tincta culpas diluit.

John Colet was another of the friends who availed himself
of Erasmus's willingness to versify; and perhaps most interesting, to English readers, of all the great Humanist's poems
is the distich which he wrote to be inscribed beneath the
image of the child Jesus in St. Paul's School:

Discite me primum, pueri, atque effingite puris
Moribus; inde pias addite literulas.
(First learn of me, scholars, and attain to pure man-
ners; then add your devout literary studies.)

Other inscriptions which Erasmus composed for other
places in Colet's school may be read in Knight's *Life of
Colet* (1823).

≺ II ≻

OUR history of epigram-writing properly begins with Sir
Thomas More.[12] Through his connections with Linacre, Grocyn, and Colet, as well as by his own studies, More is identi-

---

[12] The work of the mediaeval Latin epigrammatists of England (such as
Godfrey of Winchester and Henry of Huntingdon, whose work will be
found in *Anglo-Latin Satirical Poets and Epigrammatists of the Twelfth
Century*, collected by Thomas Wright, 1872) seems to have had no influence upon epigram-writing in later periods. Tucker (*Verse-Satire in
England Before the Renaissance*) does not treat of them, saying (p. 17n)
"their Epigrams, scholarly imitations of those of Martial, form 'an isolated
phenomenon.' " With More we are virtually at the entrance of the epigram into English literature. It is noteworthy that Charles Fitzgeoffrey, in
his Latin epigrams (*Affaniae*, 1601), refers to More as the first to write
such poems in England, naming Campion as the second. For Latin epigrams by mediaeval English writers see also *Anecdota Oxoniensa*, I (1885),
Part V, "Harleian Ms. 2610 . . . XXIV, Latin Epigrams from Bodleian or
other Mss.," edited by Robinson Ellis.
˜ See also Thomas Wright, *Political Poems and Songs Relating to English
History* (1859, Rerum Britannicarum Medii Aevi Scriptores, XIV), I, 26 and
II, 127, 130, 253, for Latin epigrams from the fourteenth century.

fied with that early English Humanism which bore such abundant fruit in the Age of Elizabeth. Through his own travels and his friendship with Erasmus he connects with the great body of European scholars, with whom epigram-writing was a diversion and an accomplishment. And through quotation, translation, and imitation the influence of More's epigrams was present in England throughout the period we are considering.

In an address prefatory to More's published *Epigrammata* (1518), Beatus Rhenanus, a renowned German scholar, paid to the poems a tribute of which the following represents a part:

"Thomas More is marvelous in everie respect; for he compoundeth most eloquently, and translateth most happily: how sweetly doe his verses flowe from him! how nothing in them seemeth constrained! how easie are all things there that he speaketh of! nothing is hard, nothing rugged, nothing obscure; he is pure, he is wittie, he is elegant; besides he doth temper all things with mirth, as that I never read a merrier man. I could thinke that the Muses have heaped upon him alone all their pleasant conceipts and wittie merriments; moreover his quippes are not biting, but full of pleasantness and verie proper, yea rather anie thing than stinging; for he ieasteth, but without mordacitie; he scoffeth, yet without contumelie."[13]

A still higher tribute, perhaps, was that of Leger Du-chesne (or du Chêne), known to the scholarly world as Leodegarius a Quercu, who included in his anthology of Neo-Latin epigrams, *Flores Epigrammatum* (Paris, 1555),

---

[13] The translation is by Cresacre More, great-grandson of Sir Thomas, in his *Life and Death of Sir Thomas Moore*, 1631; I quote from the edition of 1726, p. 12. This tribute was also included by Stapleton in his well-known life of More in *Tres Thomae* (Douai, 1588); see the translation by Philip E. Hallett, *The Life and Illustrious Martyrdom of Sir Thomas More* (1928), p. 7.

a larger number of selections from More than from any other writer. Eighty-three poems by More appear in the section headed by his name in the *Flores Epigrammatum*. But among the translations from the Greek Anthology Duchesne includes sixty-two of More's Latin versions, crediting them to him by name. Except for this last circumstance, we should have to point out that Duchesne is an anthologist who printed more selections from his own works than from any other author. At any rate, it is not strange that Francis Meres, in his chapter of *Palladis Tamia* (1598) treating "Of Poetry and Poets," lists More with the great Latin epigrammatists of all time. "The Latin tongue," says Meres, speaking of epigrammatists, "hath Q. Catulus, Porcus Licinius, Quintus Cornificius, Martial, Cnœus Getulicus, and wittie Sir Thomas Moore."

More's epigram-writing began, as did that of many of the authors we shall consider, in his school days. Cresacre More writes: "When this towardlie youth was come to the age of eighteen yeares, he beganne to shew to the world his ripeness of witt; for he wrote many wittie and goodlie Epigrammes. . . ."[14] Some of his translations from Greek to Latin may be supposed to have been student exercises. Erasmus tells us of More: "When he was very young, he amused himself with Epigrams, most of them being written when he was still a boy."[15] Among his earliest composi-

~~~~~~~~~~

[14] *Op. cit.*, p. 11.

[15] In his epistle to John Froben, printed in the Basel (1518) edition of the *Utopia*, with which More's epigrams appeared; translated in Nichols, *Epistles of Erasmus*, III, 22. We may safely discount the statement of Erasmus, echoed by later biographers, that *most* of More's epigrams belong to his boyhood. This seems to be colored by the desire to emphasize More's precocity. As a matter of fact, the epigrams contain numerous allusions which help in dating them; and this dating has been worked out with some care by Georg Thomas Rudhart in his *Thomas Morus* (2d ed.; Augsburg, 1852), showing that their composition extended over some twenty years. A few were written between 1518, when they were first published,

tions may certainly be placed the English verses which, according to the collectors of his *Workes* (1557), were written in his youth to be placed over nine pictures, or "pageants," on the painted cloth in a room of his father's house, —"which verses expressed and declared, what the ymages in those pageauntes represented." This series consists of eight stanzas of seven lines each, riming after the pattern of the then common *rime royal*, and a ninth of twelve Latin verses. The subjects of the first eight are: Childhood, Manhood, Venus and Cupid, Age, Death, Fame, Time, and Eternity. The ninth is upon the Poet. Let us choose, as a specimen, the verses upon Age, transcribing the introductory note of the first editors:

"In the fourth pageaunt was paynted an olde sage father sittyng in a chayre. And lyeng under his fete was painted the ymage of Venus and Cupyde, that were in the third pageaunt. And ouer this fourth pageaunt the scripture was thus."

AGE

Olde Age am I, with lokkes thynne and hore,
Of our short lyfe the last and best part
Wyse and dyscrete: the publike wele therefore,
I helpe to rule to my labour and smart,
Therefore Cupyde withdraw thy fyry dart,
Chargeable matters shall of loue oppresse,
Thy childish game and ydle bysinesse.[16]

Although these sets of verses are reprinted by Flügel under his heading "Das Epigram," I am inclined to classify them rather as emblems, admitting that the emblem falls

and 1520, the date of the second edition. More was forty years of age in 1518.

[16] The series is reprinted from the 1557 edition by Flügel, *Neuenglisches Lesebuch* (Halle, 1895), I, 40 ff., and (modernized) in *Utopia and Poems by Sir Thomas More* (Methuen Standard Library, 1906).

within the scope of epigrammatic poetry, broadly considered. The emblem is easy to recognize, since it accompanies an allegorical or a symbolical picture; and its purpose is to point out the "lesson" of the picture. It is, to be sure, a kind of inscription, but its allegorical, symbolical, and homiletic nature set it apart from the true epigram. In practice, the two are not often confused. Francis Quarles wrote both emblems and epigrams, but he kept them fairly distinct; and the same statement holds for Francis Thynne and for Henry Peacham. Thynne had no pictures prepared for his emblems, and realizing the importance of the omission he apologized for presenting them "naked (for soe I doe terme them, because they are not clothed with engraven pictures)."[17]

"An emblem is but a silent Parable," said Francis Quarles. The definition by Bacon (*Advancement of Learning*, Book V, Chap. 5) likewise emphasizes the didactic nature of the emblem and makes it nearly synonymous with our term "object-lesson": "*Embleme* deduceth conceptions intellectual to images sensible, and that which is sensible more forcibly strikes the memory, and is more easily imprinted than that which is intellectual." *The Arte of English Poesie* (1589) does not connect emblems and epigrams at all, but treats of emblems in a separate chapter. His explanation of emblems follows:

"These be the short, quicke and sententious propositions, such as be at these days all your devices of armes and other amorous inscriptions which courtiers use to give and also to weare in liverie for the honour of their ladies, and commonly contain but two or three words of wittie sentence or secret conceit till they unfolded [*sic*] or explained by some interpretation. For which cause they be commonly accom-

---

[17] *Emblemes and Epigrames*, prepared for publication, 1600; printed by the Early English Text Society (ed. Furnivall, 1876), p. 2.

panied with a figure or purtrait of ocular representation, the words so aptly corresponding to the subtilitie of the figure, that aswel the eye is therewith recreated as the eare or the mind. The Greekes call it *Emblema*, the Italiens, *Impresa*, and we, a Device. . . ."

"Puttenham" is undoubtedly correct in identifying the emblem with the impresa, or device;[18] but he could not have been familiar with emblem-books or he would have known that the emblem had developed as a form separate from the *impresa*, and rarely consisted of "but two or three words." The subject of More's emblems, the division of man's life into periods, with some specification of his changing interests, was not unknown in earlier emblem-literature.[19]

[18] The *impresa*, or device, was usually a verse or motto for a coat of arms; it bears the same relation to the coat of arms as the emblem to the picture accompanying it.

[19] See Henry Green, *Shakespeare and the Emblem-Writers* (1870), pp. 407-410; or better, John Winter Jones, "Observations on the Origin of the Division of Man's Life into Stages," *Archaeologia*, xxxv, 167. In the Dutch version (Harlem, 1485) of *De Proprietatibus Rerum* by Bartholomaeus Anglicus, there is a woodcut showing seven figures: "a naked child, a small boy with a whirligig, a youth with a bow, a young man with a falcon, and three men more advanced in years standing in a group. . . . Last of all, a corpse lies on the ground." (Campbell Dodgson, *Catalogue of German and Flemish Woodcuts*, I, 225.)

That the "seven ages of man" (but only six ages of women) were actually a continuate part of popular lore is also evidenced by these entries in Egerton MS. 2642, a miscellaneous collection dating from about the beginning of Elizabeth's reign:

(fol. 269r) Septem sunt Ætates in hominem

1	Infans	vii annos
2	Puer	xiiii annos
3	Adolescens	xxviii annos
4	Iuventus	xl annos
5	Vir	lx annos
6	Senectus	lxxviii annos
7	Decrepitus	vsque ad finem vitae.

VERSUS

Infans, inde puer, adolescens, post iuvenis vir
Dicitur homo, senex, postea Decrepitus.

Several commentators have found a significant resemblance between these emblems by More and the "seven ages" of Jaques (*As You Like It*, II, vii). The underlying idea and some of the details employed both by More and Shakespeare derive, it may be said, from originals which were old and fairly common when More wrote. However, the series of pictures moralized by More, as we learn from the notes printed with his verses, includes considerably more than the idea of the division of man's life into stages. It will be noticed that each figure in the list represents the conqueror of its predecessor—Manhood conquers Childhood, Venus and Cupid conquer Manhood, Age conquers these, Death conquers Age, Fame conquers Death, and so on. This conception, more rarely met with than that of the "seven ages," suggests the emblems (in the form of "Visions") translated by the young Spenser, with their similar emphasis upon transitoriness.

~~~~~~

                    Mans Age divided heere yee have
                    By prentishipps, from birth to grave

        7   The first vii yeares, bring vpp as a chylde
        14   The next, to Learning, or waxing to wild
        21   The next, keepe vndre for Hobble de hoye
        28   The next, a man, no longer a boy
                    etc. [complete in MS.]
        The Description of Womans Age by vi Tymes xiiii
        yeeres prentishipp with a Lesson for the same
        1[4] Twoo first vii yeeres, for a Rodde they do whyne
        28   Twoo next, as a Pearle, in the world they do shine
        42   Twoo next, trym Beauty beginneth to swerve
        56   Twoo next, for Matrons, or Drudges they serve
        70   Twoo next, doeth crave, a staffe for a staye
        84   Twoo nexte, a Beere, to fetche them a way.
                    A Lesson   Then purchase some pellfe
                               by fifty and Three
                               or buckle thy Self
                               a drudge for to bee.

≺ III ≻

THE first edition of More's *Epigrammata* was published at Basel by John Froben, in March of 1518, together with the third edition of *Utopia* and with the epigrams of Erasmus. In May of the previous year Erasmus had sent to Froben, from Antwerp, corrected copies of *Utopia* and of More's epigrams;[20] and in August he sent a letter to be printed at the beginning of the projected volume. Passages which relate to the epigrams follow:

"What indeed might not have been expected from that admirable felicity of nature, if this genius had had Italian instruction, if it had been entirely consecrated to the Muses, and had been allowed to ripen at its proper season? When he was very young, he amused himself with Epigrams, most of them being written when he was still a boy. . . .

"Hence it comes, that we have sent you his early exercises, as well as his Utopia, that, if you think fit, they may, —printed with your types,—be commended to the world and to posterity; since such is the authority of your Press, that the learned are ready to accept any book with pleasure, if it be known to have come from the house of Froben."[21] The publication was supervised by Beatus Rhenanus (1485-1547) who wrote a prefatory epistle for the *Epigrammata*, inscribing the book to Bilibald Pirckheimer, a senator of Nuremburg and himself a scholar and author. The volume was a small quarto.

This edition was reissued in November of the same year. Two years later a corrected and enlarged edition was pub-

---

[20] Allen, *Erasmi Epistolae*, II, 576; Erasmus is writing to More (here translated): "I have sent your *Epigrammata* and *Utopia* to Basel by my own servant . . . together with some of my own lucubrations." The last phrase must include Erasmus's own epigrams, which he elsewhere referred to as published by "partial friends."

[21] Translation by Nichols, *Epistles of Erasmus*, III, 21.

lished at Basel, with the title as before except for the addition, *Ad emendatum exemplar ipsius Auctoris excusa.*[22] Besides appearing, in part, in several anthologies, More's epigrams have been available to later times through their inclusion in the miscellaneous collection of his works entitled *Lucubrationes* (Basel, 1563), and through the Louvain edition of all his Latin writings, published in 1566. In 1638 appeared the first edition in England of the *Epigrammata*, the project of Humphrey Mosley. The complete Latin works were again published in 1689, at Frankfort. The *poemata* were reprinted in the nineteenth century by Arthur Cayley, at the end of his *Memoirs of Sir Thomas More* (two volumes, 1808).

At the close of his prefatory epistle, Beatus Rhenanus introduces More's friend, William Lily, in a passage which may be translated thus:

"William Lily, friend of More, with whom he worked some time since at translating the Greek epigrams which are here included under the title of *Progymnasmata*, is an Englishman of wide learning, who not only knows the Greek authors but also has a familiar acquaintance with the indigenous customs of that nation; for he had sojourned for some years in the Isle of Rhodes. He now teaches, with great success, in the grammar-school which Colet founded in London."

The *Progymnasmata* of Thomas More and William Lily, *sodalium,* follow immediately. These consist of eight-

---

[22] Twice in the edition of 1518 two epigrams were printed as one; these are separated in 1520. The two translations from English songs (discussed *infra*) were not so designated in 1518. The monostich concerning Homer (translated from the Greek Anthology) first appears in 1520, as do eleven miscellaneous poems at the end of the volume. The first edition ended with More's epitaph upon his wives and himself. Two poems appearing in 1518 were omitted from the edition of 1520: one is a two-line variant translation of the Greek epigram, *In piscatorem adamatum*; the other is a twelve-line poem *In Jacobum Regem Scotorum.*

een epigrams from the Greek Anthology, each with Latin versions by Lily and More.[23] The word *progymnasmata*, "preparatory exercises," was used for schoolboys' assignments; for this reason, with some others, commentators have usually ascribed these translations to the early youth of these two men. But the school days of the two by no means coincided, and Lily, having taken his Oxford degree, was abroad in Rhodes and Italy while More was in his teens. Hence it is more probable that More was at least twenty years old and Lily at least thirty when they engaged in these exercises. The epigrams they chose for translation are about one-third satirical, one-third "admonitory" or moralistic, and one-third "declamatory." Later we shall meet some of these same epigrams in English—and in more than one instance translated from the Latin of Lily or More rather than from the original Greek.

For the present, let us dwell for a moment upon the story of one of them, a story which will show how the translation of a Greek epigram could pass into currency as a commonplace of European thought. The epigram in Greek is a distich of unknown authorship:

Ἐλπὶς καὶ σύ, Τύχη, μεγα χαίρετε . τον λιμέν' εὗρον·
οὐδὲν ἐμοί χ' ὑμῖν· παίζετε τοὺς μετ' ἐμέ.

(Farewell, Hope and Fortune, a long farewell. I have found the haven. I have no more to do with you. Make game of those who come after me.)[24]

The translations by More and Lily are almost identical:

---

[23] "Morant, who wrote Lilye's Life in the old *Biographia*, says that in this epigrammatical contest, Lilye appears, upon the whole, to outdo Sir Thomas More." Wood, *Athenae Oxoniensis*, ed. Bliss, I, 38.

[24] III, 26, 27. (All references to the Greek Anthology are to the edition in the Loeb Classical Library, with an English translation by W. R. Paton, *by volume and page*.)

T. MORI DE CONTEMTU FORTUNAE

Jam portum inveni, Spes et Fortuna valete,
Nil mihi vobiscum est, ludite nunc alios.

G. LILII

Inveni portum, Spes et Fortuna valete,
Nil mihi vobiscum, ludite nunc alios.

But these young men were not the only ones who had
turned this epigram into Latin. A translation identical with
that of Lily is found at the conclusion of the epitaph inscribed on the tomb of Francisco Pucci at Rome. Pucci died
in 1512. Earlier than this, Janus Pannonius (Joannes Ce-
singe), Bishop of Fünfkirchen, in Hungary, had made or
recorded this identical translation; but the version was not
published from his manuscript until 1569, though he died
in 1472. Shortly after its appearance in More's *Epigrammata*, the couplet was included in the *Epigrammata* of Johannes Soter (Cologne, 1525). Again it was printed, as
copied from Pucci's tomb, in the *Variorum in Europa Itin-
erum Deliciae* of Nathan Chytraeus, published in 1594, and
in *Select. Christiani Orbis Deliciis*, compiled by Franciscus
Sweertius and published in 1626. John Weever found the
distich, exactly as credited to Lily, in the church at Barking,
Essex, "under the picture of a ship sailing into the haven."
Weever's record is found in his *Antient Funeral Monuments* (1631). Another antiquarian[25] found the lines engraved on the tomb of Roland Meyric (d. 1565), at Bangor.
And we learn from Egerton MS. 2642 (fol. 216r) that Bartholomew Green, the Protestant martyr, had sent an English translation of this epigram to William Fleetwood, Re-
corder of London, while Green was awaiting execution by
burning in 1556. This translation, one of our earliest English versions of a Greek epigram, follows:

[25] Humphreys, in Wood's *Athenae Oxoniensis*, ed. Bliss, II, 799.

My resting Roade is proude [proved]
Vayne hope and happe adewe
Lowte whome you lyste with chaunge
Deathe shall me ryd from you.

By this time, evidently, the couplet had become a rhetorical commonplace. Thus in Walter Haddon's *Poemata* (1567) is an epitaph, *In obitum N. Pointzi, Equitis*, which contains the line,

Nunc teneo portum, valeant ludibria mundi.

Haddon's verses are a translation from the English of Thomas Henneage; and in the English the connection with the Greek epigram may have appeared still more close. Again, Sir Walter Ralegh, writing to Sir Robert Cecil in July, 1592, a time of deep trouble for Ralegh, uses the exclamation, "Spes et fortuna, valete!" Thomas Lodge, in his *Life and Death of William Longbeard* (1593) quoted Lily's couplet as the inscription which "Porides the Athenian" (Pericles?) placed above the door of his house after retiring from public service. Robert Burton quoted the couplet and gave an English translation of it in *The Anatomy of Melancholy* (1621), mentioning that the lines come from the tomb of Puccius and also are to be found in Prudentius.[26] And George Sandys used an abridgement of the first line at the end of his *Divine Poems* (1638): *Jam tetigi Portum,—valete*. Anthony à Wood quoted the couplet, but mistakenly connected it with the tomb of another Pucci at Salzburg.[27]

We need not follow this epigram beyond the seventeenth century. But it is interesting to find it used, with a slight change in the second line, by Le Sage in *Gil Blas* (1735); and again, with the insertion of *est* in the second line, in

[26] Part II, sect. iii, memb. 6. Burton seems to have been wrong in connecting the couplet with Prudentius.
[27] *Athenae Oxoniensis*, I, 589.

Casanova's *Memoires*. According to Casanova it was a translation, made by his teacher, from a couplet in Euripides.[28] How much Lily and More had to do with putting this epigram into currency, we do not know. We can say, however, that the version which became most popular appears in no printed book earlier than More's *Epigrammata*; and there it is attributed to William Lily.

◅ IV ►

At the beginning of the *epigrammata* proper stand the five poems written by More at the time of the marriage and accession of Henry VIII, and presented to the King in an illuminated booklet.[29] The first and longest piece, called by its author *Carmen gratulorum*, is an ode rather than an epigram. Of the other four, three may be called epigrams; the last is the celebrated one on the union of the Red and White Roses,[30] "which," says a modern reader, "unless it is condemned on the score of lacking brevity, is happier than most which we can recall. In twelve lines Sir Thomas contrives to turn at least half-a-dozen pretty compliments; winding up all with a suggestion to such as are not content to acquiesce in the settlement of differences between the Houses of York and Lancaster that the new parti-colored Rose is one which has its thorns, and that the disaffected

~~~~~~~~~~

[28] *Memoires* (Paris, 1882), IV, 297. The foregoing account of this epigram has been gleaned principally from *Notes and Queries*, 9th series, II, 41 (and earlier references there listed); 10th series, IX, 324; *Gentleman's Magazine*, 1816, II, 160, 194, 422. An early contributor to *Notes and Queries* (6th series, IV, 76) gives other Latin versions of the epigram, saying that, in various forms, it was a common sepulchral inscription among the Romans.

[29] Now in the British Museum, Cotton MSS., Titus D iv.

[30] An English verse-rendering by Thomas Pecke (*Parnassi Puerperium*, 1659) is given in Dodd, *The Epigrammatists* (1876), p. 113.

will have to heed the argument of fear, if they regard not that of love."[31]

Translations from the Greek are scattered throughout the volume. Some seventy epigrams (apart from those of the *Progymnasmata*) are headed "e Graeco." But as with later writers we shall consider, More was not scrupulous to acknowledge all debts, and some borrowings from the Greek are unmarked. Among these are seven versions of the well-known epigrams concerning the blind beggar who arranged to furnish legs in exchange for using the sight of a lame beggar; perhaps More assumed that any reader of Latin would know that these were translations. Again, we find in More this distich:

> In Mortis Diem Omnibus Incertum
> Non ego quos rapuit mors, defleo, defleo vivos,
> Quos urunt longo fata futura metu.

This seems to be a version of an anonymous Greek epigram which has thus been translated:

> I lament no longer those who have left the sweet daylight, but those who ever live in expectation of death.[32]

Some of More's pieces are imitations rather than translations of Greek originals, wherein he borrows a thought and builds about it a new epigram. These are not always easy to identify, but an instance or two may be cited. More writes "On a Ridiculous Astrologer," translated thus by Pecke (1659):

---

[31] James Davies, *Quarterly Review*, cxvii (1865), 236.

[32] Paton, iv, pp. 202, 203; William Cowper translated this epigram, *Works* (Globe edition), p. 501. In *Quaternio* (1633), p. 192, by Thomas Nashe (not the playwright and pamphleteer), More's Latin is quoted with no reference to a Greek original.

> Cumaean Sybils could not more descry,
> Although enlightned from Divinity;
> Than our astrologer: whose profound Art,
> Could through the Stars, a thing, when past, impart.

It has been pointed out[33] that this imitates an epigram by Lucilius, elsewhere Latinized by More, which runs thus in English prose:

> All the astrologers as it were with one voice prophesied to my father a ripe old age for his brother. Hermoclides alone foretold his premature death, but he foretold it when we were lamenting over his corpse in the house.[34]

Similarly, we find More translating from the Greek what he calls "Sententia Aristotelis," to the effect that in sleep the rich King Croesus is no happier than the beggar Irus. He follows this with "Aliud"—another version of the same idea, less specific. A little below these he places a poem entitled, "Tyrannum in Somno Nihil diferre a plebejo," and somewhat later appears "De somno aequante pauperem cum divite." Again, More's epigram on Nicolaus, an ignorant physician who slew as many with drugs and potions as a general slew in battle, is an imitation of one by Lucilius which compares the fatal powers of a physician and a bad poet with those of Deucalion's flood and Phaethon's drouth.[35]

Little need be said concerning the subjects of the epigrams More chose to translate. We find here a score of trifles which have become, through translation and quotation, familiar in English literature—the aged Lais to her useless looking-

---

[33] Dodd, *The Epigrammatists* (1876), p. 113; but Dodd failed to notice that More had also translated the Greek epigram here imitated.

[34] Paton, IV, 149.

[35] Dodd, *The Epigrammatists*, p. 114. For the Greek epigram, see Paton, IV, 134, 135; for More's, Cayley, *Memoirs*, II, 298.

glass, the viper who bit the Cappadocian and died, the slave who, being dead, is the equal of King Darius, the man with the inordinately large nose, the little man who hanged himself with a spider's web, and so on. More's skill in making verse-translations appears to have been adequate, though not extraordinary. In the following, he has managed to find words of similar sound to use in the antithesis of the second line—a device dear to epigrammatists; he is translating a distich attributed to Plato:

> Naufragus hac situs est, jacet illa rusticus urna,
> Ad styga sive solo par via, sive salo.[36]

More was one of those fortunate individuals who catch the sense of a passage in a foreign tongue, not by analysis, but, as by intuition, from the whole. This fact was testified to contemporaneously by Richard Pace in his book *De Fructu qui ex Doctrina* (Basel, 1517); his comment has thus been Englished:

"Here I will remark that no one ever lived who did not first ascertain the meaning of words, and from them gather the meaning of the sentences which they compose—no one, I say, with one single exception, and that is our own Thomas More. For he is wont to gather the force of words from the sentences in which they occur, especially in his study and translation of Greek. This is not contrary to grammar, but above it, and an instinct of genius."[37]

More owed to the Greek Anthology some eighty-five of his poems—more than one-third of the two hundred and fifty which constitute the *epigrammata* proper.[38] Deducting

~~~~~~~~~~

[36] Paton, ii, 146, 147. Paton translates the Greek: "I am the tomb of a shipwrecked man, and that opposite is the tomb of a husbandman. So death lies in wait for us alike on sea and land."

[37] Thomas E. Bridgett, *Life and Writings of Blessed Thomas More* (1891), p. 12.

[38] Not "barely one-fourth," as Marsden found (*Philomorus*, p. 18).

non-epigrammatic poems, we have left over one hundred and fifty epigrams to be attributed to him. These will fall, with one or two exceptions, into the classes of admonitory, commendatory, satirical (by far the largest class), and sepulchral. The admonitory include those such as "Vita Brevis," "Ad Contemptum Hujus Vitae," and "Vita Ipsa Cursus ad mortem est." Several in this class, of special interest on account of More's public career, embody a political thought. Such are "De Bono Rege et populo" and "Populis Consentiens Regnum dat et aufert." The last line of the epigram "De Gloria, et Populi Judicio,"

> Articulus doleat, quid tibi fama facit?

("Your finger aches,—what can fame do for you?") has been mentioned [39] as an anticipation of Falstaff's "catechism" (*2 Henry* IV, v, i):

> ... Can honor set to a leg? no: or an arm? no: or take away the grief of a wound? no. Honor hath no skill in surgery, then? no. ...

Another of these moralistic epigrams restates an old thought concerning prayer:

> Quod paucis Orandus Deus
> Da bona sive rogere Deus, seu nulla rogere.
> Et mala sive rogere nega, seu nulla rogere.

(Send blessings, Lord, whether we ask them or not; and deny evils, whether we ask them or not.)

Shakespeare repeats this thought in *Antony and Cleopatra* (II, i, 5-8):

> We, ignorant of ourselves,
> Beg often our own harms, which the wise powers
> Deny us for our good; so we find profit
> By losing of our prayers.

---

[39] *Philomorus*, p. 190.

The couplet entitled "Patientia,"

> Tristia qui pateris, perfer: Sors tristia solvet.
> Quod si non faciat Sors, tibi mors faciet,

has been put into English thus:

> Bear grief with patience. Fortune will amend.
> If Fortune mend not, death will soon it end.[40]

Among the commendatory epigrams we should notice three concerning Erasmus's *editio princeps* of the Greek New Testament (with his own Latin translation), which came from Froben's printing-office early in 1516. More wrote a tribute addressed to the reader, a commendatory epigram addressed to the Reverend Thomas, Cardinal, and Archbishop of York (Wolsey), and another to the Archbishop of Canterbury (Warham). The two last accompanied copies sent as gifts by Erasmus. Three other epigrams relate to Jerome Busleiden, a scholar and prelate of Malines (Mechlin), at whose home More had stayed while he was on a diplomatic mission in Flanders in 1515. Soon after returning, he had written to Erasmus: "Another circumstance was my acquaintance with Busleiden, who entertained me with a magnificence suitable to his noble fortune, and a kindness proportioned to the goodness of his heart. He showed me a house adorned with singular taste and provided with the choicest furniture; he showed me many monuments of antiquity, of which you know I am curious, and finally his well-stored library, and a mind still better stored."[41] The epigrams enforce the sentiments of the letter. One of them is about the collection of coins owned by Busleiden; the second reproaches him because he does not publish his

---

[40] "A contemporaneous translation," says Marsden, *Philomorus*, p. 188.

[41] Nichols, *Epistles of Erasmus*, II, 260-261. Epitaphs upon Busleiden by Erasmus, written in Greek and Latin, may be seen in Allen, *Erasmi Epistolae*, III, 124, 258-259. Busleiden died in 1517, but evidently too late for More to take any notice of his death in the *Epigrammata*.

poems; the third commends his magnificent house at Malines. This last has been summarized as follows:

> Your mansion is so well arranged in all its compartments that it surely must have been the contrivance of Daedalus. You appear to have prevailed upon the fates to restore to life all the great artists of antiquity. Your sculptures, paintings, casts, and carvings seem to be the work of Praxiteles, Apelles, Lysippus, and Myron; while the distich to each appended is such as might have excited the jealousy of Maro himself. Everything about you savours of classical antiquity excepting your organ; and that it would have been beyond the power of antiquity to produce.[42]

Another laudatory epigram was occasioned by the fall of Tournay, in 1513, before the arms of Henry VIII. The English king is compared to Julius Caesar, with disadvantage to Caesar.

≺ V ≻

MORE's satirical epigrams ring the changes on themes old as the Greek epigrammatists and Martial, themes which recur throughout the epigram-writing of all nations. He deserves some credit for stressing one subject which few satirists have hit upon, namely, cruelty toward animals, especially as practised by hunters. For the rest, he directs his ridicule toward drunkards, physicians, misers, poetasters, painters, astrologers, spendthrifts, soldiers, courtiers, women, and priests. With the epigrammatists the question must be asked, as it has been asked concerning writers of sonnet-cycles: are their products wholly conventional exercises, or do they grow out of actual experiences? In the work of

---

[42] *Philomorus*, pp. 86-87, slightly altered in the opening. The reference to a distich appended to each statue and painting suggests the great demand there must have been for epigrammatic poems for such uses.

More, we find evidence that many of his epigrams are the genuine expression of his daily life and thought.[43] We have noticed the parallel between his letter to Erasmus and his epigrams upon Busleiden. His political epigrams, already mentioned, express views that are stated in *Utopia* and in his speeches. Evidence cited by his biographers as to his fondness for animals proves the sincerity of his epigrams against hunting. Again, in *Utopia* and elsewhere we find More ridiculing a method of argument used by monks and priests which consists of quoting some one text to support any point. So in the *Epigrammata* we find a poem, "In Episcopum Illiteratim," about a bishop whose favorite text was, "The letter killeth." This epigram was translated by Francis Thynne, who included the translation (without credit to More) in his manuscript *Emblemes and Epigrames* (1600):

> A preist which knewe not anie letter.
> Of holie Pawle, yet thow the heavenlie voice
> cannst ringe alowd, and sound this sentence true,
> 'the Letter kills,' wherby thow maiest reioyse,
> that of one Letter the forme thow never knew.
> ffor least that this dead letter should thee kill,
> thow didst beware the letters for to learne,
> and that aptlie, since of gods holie will
> the quickning spirit thow never couldst deserne.[44]

---

[43] "When Sir Thomas More held the office of Under-sheriff in the City of London he would know something of the city banquets. Hence an epigramma which is thus translated by Kendall:—

> When Eutiches doth run a race
> He seems to stand, perdy!
> But when he runs unto a feast,
> Then sure he seems to fly."

So Marsden, in *Philomorus*, p. 237. The epigram cited, however, was one of More's translations from the Greek (Paton, IV, 170, 171). This fact does not invalidate the suggestion of Marsden. As with sonneteers, we may assume that epigrammatists often took over from the classics a thought or an expression which fitted the circumstances of their own lives.

[44] Early English Text Society, 1876, p. 60. I have omitted four lines of introduction, added by Thynne.

Similarly, More writes a spirited quatrain "On a certain fat priest who frequently quoted, 'Knowledge puffeth up.' "[45]

We may also consider in this connection a group of epigrams by which More precipitated himself into a literary controversy with Germain de Brie,[46] a French writer of Latin poetry, whom we may call by his Latinized name of Brixius. The story begins with a naval engagement on August 10, 1512, outside the harbor of Brest, where Sir Edward Howard with a fleet of eighteen ships had come upon a fleet of thirty-five Frenchmen. H. A. L. Fisher gives this account:

"The *Regent* and the *Cordeliere*, the first of 1000 and the second of some 700 tons, came into collision, while the majority of the French fleet sped away into the safe recesses of the harbour. English archers and French crossbowmen interchanged a hot fire, and then the *Regent's* crew boarded the Frenchman. Suddenly—no one knows how—the French powder-magazine blew up, and both ships were involved in flame. Porzmoguer, the French captain, jumped into the sea with his armour and was drowned, and Sir Thomas Knyvet, captain of the *Regent*, perished likewise with the greater part of his crew. The destruction of these two noble vessels, locked in deadly embrace, and sinking with their gallant crews in a consuming fury of smoke and fire, was the great tragedy of the war. . . . Howard vowed that he would never look the king in the face till he had avenged the death of

[45] Literally translated, More says: " 'Knowledge puffeth up,' you say on Paul's authority; 'flee from it.' Wherefore then do you, father, swell so corpulently? You can scarcely carry about your swelling middle with its fat paunch,—and your light mind is puffed up with ignorance."

[46] Sometimes called Germain Brice; his chief volume of poems was printed in 1519, after which time he devoted himself to theology. He was for a time King's almoner and then Canon of the Cathedral of Paris. This statement from a biographical dictionary, concerning his death, may throw light upon the temperament which made him a controversialist with More: "il mourut en 1538, dans le diocese de Chartres, de chagrin, dit-on, d'avoir été volé."

Sir Thomas Knyvet. Two days after the engagement the English landed, captured five and burnt twenty-seven French vessels, and took 800 prisoners."[47]

The full name of the luckless French captain was Hervé Porzmoguer. The poet Brixius made Hervé an epic hero in the Latin poem of three hundred and fifty verses which he wrote to memorialize the encounter, *Herveus, sive Chordigera Flagrans*, 1513. The account given by Brixius differs from that of Mr. Fisher in representing Hervé and his men as aggressors throughout and victors, though they perished, at the end.

When Thomas More read *Herveus* he resented the slurs cast by Brixius upon English honor, not to mention the extravagance of certain passages lauding the French commander. In protest he composed a number of epigrams for circulation among his friends. He knew that these scoffing poems had danger in them; and when, in 1517, publication of his *epigrammata* was in prospect, he wrote thus to Erasmus:

"If you publish my *Epigrammata*, please consider whether the verses I wrote against De Brie ought to be suppressed, as containing some things over bitter, although I might seem to have received provocation from him in the reproaches uttered against my country. Nevertheless, as I have said, please consider this matter; and in fact dispose of everything you may think invidious or merely silly, in such a way as you think best for me."[48]

Erasmus allowed nine poems against Brixius to pass to the press. The first two directly attack the veracity of *Herveus* as an account of the engagement, with special reference to slurs upon English valor. Then More quotes two passages from Brixius' poem, to this effect:

---

[47] *The History of England (1485-1547)*, 1906, p. 177.
[48] Nichols, *Epistles of Erasmus*, II, 382.

"The British came about Hervé from the right and left at once; weapons flew thicker than hail in winter against his head, but the hero, boldly warding them off with his shield, turned them into the ranks of his foe. . . .

"Hervé himself exhorted his comrades and pressed on: bravely, among the first, he attacked the foe in great force: he smote some with a dart driven through the temples, another he pierced through the ribs with a sword, for another he cut open the groin, of some he cut off the head with a stroke of his axe on the neck, of these the belly, of those the shoulders he pricked with his keen spear."

More now speaks:

"It is a matter of record that Hervé smote some with a dart driven through the temples, and he pierced groins and ribs with a sword, he cut off the head of some with a stroke of his axe on the neck, he perforated shoulders and bellies with a spear, while with a shield he was bravely warding off flying missiles and turning them toward the foe. This escapes comprehension, that one man should be fighting with so many weapons—and he has a shield weighing down one hand. The steadfast nature of things is repugnant to such fighting; and I am inclined to think something got away from you in this passage. Where you brought on the great-souled Hervé fighting with four weapons at once, and with a shield, perchance you overlooked the fact that the reader should have been informed that Hervé had five hands."

And again:

"You wonder that Hervé wields sword, shield, spear, dart, axe, and thus goes on fighting. His right hand is weaponed with the cruel axe, while his dangerous left is furnished with a sword. Now the dart, and that which serves as a dart, the spear, he stoutly holds in his mouth, clamping his teeth on them. But since missiles are flying against his head thicker than hail in winter, he puts his shield on his head. . . ."

[51]

Then More turns to a passage wherein Brixius represents Hervé as making a prophetic speech before his death, saying in it, among other things, that some one of the foster-sons of Apollo (*i.e.*, poets) would not disdain to give eternal fame to the day's business. In other words, Brixius represents himself as writing *Herveus* practically by request of its hero. More's epigram on this extravagance consists of four distichs, each of which mockingly begins with Brixius's words, *Inter Phoebeos non aspernandus alumnos*. The point of the epigram is made in the alternate lines, by asking: "Since all on the ship perished, whence did the bard learn all this that he sings?" The most notable of the other epigrams attacks Brixius for borrowing phrases from classical poets.

The retort of Brixius to these nine epigrams printed in 1518 took the form of a Latin poem, usually called *Antimorus*, longer by ninety lines than the *Herveus* itself. The full title is: *In Thomam Morum, Chordigerae calumniatorem, Antimorus, silua.*[49] News that the poem was being composed reached Erasmus, who at once wrote to Brixius and begged that he would not publish it. More's epigrams, he pointed out, were written during the heat of war-time. He also held up to Brixius the personal worth of More and his value as a possible friend. But according to Brixius this letter of Erasmus's, which might have served its writer's good purpose, did not arrive until *Antimorus* was in the press. The book appeared late in 1519.[50] "You say that I savor too much

---

[49] Reprinted in 1555 in *Flores Epigrammatum*, collected by Leodegarius a Quercu and printed at Paris; and again in Gruter's *Delitiae Poetarum Gallorum* (Frankfort, 1612), Vol. 1.

[50] There is some confusion in the dating of the incidents here summarized. Erasmus's letter asking Brixius to refrain from attacking More is dated by editors as written in July or August, 1517 (Nichols, *Epistles of Erasmus*, II, 578; Allen, *Erasmi Epistolae*, III, 41). If this dating is correct, then Brixius was preparing his answer before More's epigrams had been printed. This is certainly conceivable, as they circulated in manuscript. What is harder to understand is the reason why Erasmus, if he wished to

of the ancient poets," it begins; "well, no one can say that
about you! For your effusions, unless I am badly mistaken,
savor of the poets produced by your own land of Utopia."
Then More is censured for his bad Latinity and faulty verses.
"Who will not call you the English versifier whose rhythm
is framed without meter?" Errors and solecisms in More's
poetry are as numerous as the waves on the sea, the blades
of grass in the spring, the leaves in autumn. To charges of
inveracity in *Herveus* Brixius replies that evidently More
never has heard of poetic fictions—he would accuse Homer
and Virgil of lying. But that Hervé and his men did attack
the English and come off victors is true.

Brixius glances at some of More's own poems. The ode
upon Henry's accession comes first under review. "Ancient
writers say that Nicocles gave Isocrates twenty talents for a
pamphlet; so doubtless Henry gave his More a thousand
talents for a metrical poem." Brixius charges that More, in
expressing such delight at the accession of Henry VIII, went
out of his way to insult that king's predecessor and father.
And there was, of course, something in this charge. Turning
to another poem, Brixius says: "And presently, if you
please, O keen-sighted poet, you have dared to carp at a
certain Andrew, who, in composing festival hymns in
rhythm and song, said that he was not bound to the regular
meter of verse. This aberration he has in common with you,

---

forestall Brixius's attack, did not suppress the epigrams—More having
given him complete authority in the matter—which, though forwarded to
Basel in May of 1517, did not appear until March of 1518. Perhaps Erasmus, without information from Basel, supposed their printing to have
proceeded farther than it really had.

Be that as it may be, Brixius claims that he did not receive Erasmus's
letter of protest, but first read it in the published *Farrago Nova Epistolarum*
of October, 1519. By that time *Antimorus* was in the press; but Brixius
immediately appended to his poem this epistle of Erasmus's with a reply
of his own, explaining the circumstances. In the *Farrago*, incidentally,
Erasmus's epistle is dated 1518.

except that Andrew was conscious, you are unconscious, of it. . . . You never had committed such foul errors, if you had submitted your work to your friends." There follows a list of friends, including Tunstall, Pace, Linacre, and Erasmus, who might have corrected More's verses. After many other reproaches, Brixius comes to More's riming epitaph on Henry Abingdon. "*Hic iacet Henricus*—if anyone wants to know all the delights of poetry in one poem, let him read that epigram as a whole!" And if More protests that the poem is jocular,—"but lest you do not know your own good points: as a funny poet you are good; as a serious poet you are vile." The implication here, I take it, is that an epitaph actually engraved on a man's tomb should be serious. Toward the end of the poem Brixius returns to the topic of his debt to ancient authors. He challenges More to point out any instance of plagiarism; but he admits that by hard study he has mastered the classics, while More, he implies, knows none but modern authors. Then he weaves into three verses as many puns as he can make on More's name:

> Proin, si iura tui, aut patrii tibi nominis vlla est,
> More tace, aut Latio discito more loqui.
> Sicque tuos inter morari desine, More,
> Versusque, & mores, indue More nouos.

He closes with a warning to his adversary not to issue any more examples of his bad verse, and with a remark that he has been amusing himself in the *Antimorus*, writing, as it were, with his left hand.

A copy of this poem reached its subject in March of 1520. Immediately after reading it, More wrote a long letter[51] to Erasmus, complaining of Brixius's attack and making, or summarizing, some points which he contemplated using in a published reply to the poem. Erasmus, having failed in his

---

[51] Allen, *Erasmi Epistolae*, IV, 217-232.

earlier attempt to silence Brixius, now bestirred himself to
prevent the controversy's going further. On April 26 he
. addressed More from Antwerp,[52] urging his English friend
to ignore the rudeness of his French friend; he reminds
More of the fact (which More must already have known,
since the correspondence was printed with *Antimorus*) that
Brixius avows he never would have printed the offending
poem if he had received Erasmus's protest. And he says that
More's dignity will be served best by silence. To this letter
More responded, early in May,[53] with the information that
his reply to Brixius has already gone through the press; but
that the printer has sold only five copies, and that he himself
has sent out only two, one to Peter Giles and the other,
preceding his letter, to Erasmus. But he says that out of
deference to his friend he is willing to go much further than
did Brixius; he has now bought up all remaining copies of
the edition, and he will keep them hidden until he hears
further from Erasmus. He, too, is unwilling that a bitter
feud shall grow up between two of Erasmus's friends; he is
even looking forward to meeting Brixius in the near future.
"When we come to Calais, for which the king is about to
start, we will talk over the matter more at length. In this
meeting of the kings I expect you and De Brie also; since
the French queen will be there, and he, as her secretary, can
hardly be absent. So far as I am concerned you can easily
arrange the matter; for though without any reason he has
so treated me, as to show that the only thing wanting to
him for my destruction is ability, yet since you, Erasmus, are
more than half of myself, the fact that De Brie is your
friend will weigh more with me than that he is my enemy."[54]
Of the book, or pamphlet, which More has published and
engages to suppress, perhaps it is enough to translate the

[52] Allen, IV, 239.   [53] Allen, IV, 251.
[54] Translation by Bridgett, *Blessed Thomas More*, pp. 187-188.

[55]

title: "Epistle of Thomas More against Germain de Brie, who, because seven years ago More composed in sport a few epigrams against his book in which he attacked England with slanderous lies, now, in the midst of profound peace between the English and French, only six weeks before the meeting of the princes of those countries, has published a book against More, defaming that author with stupid and bitter railing." We may note also that the charge, brought by Brixius, that More had insulted the memory of Henry VII, called forth a discussion by More of that king's financial affairs, which constitutes a valuable source for historians of the times.

In the event, More proved to be either unwilling or unable to suppress the book.[55] And when, later in the year, his *Epigrammata* appeared in a second edition, there were four new epigrams against Brixius in the volume. The first of these deals with a passage, which More quotes from *Antimorus*, wherein Brixius said that while he himself was writing, the Furies appeared about him. More replies:

> Brixius had heard that many condemned him for writing falsehoods. That he might correct this fault he sought to utter something that would be true, that would be beyond doubt, that no one would deny even though Brixius wrote it. . . . One thing he discovered, more true than all else, and the charming fellow writes —that all the Furies encircle his charming head!

The next epigram is headed, "Against the ship *Chordigera* and the sylva *Antimorus* of Germanus Brixius, French-

---

[55] See Erasmus's letter to Budé, February 16, 1521 (Allen, IV, 442). At least three copies of the book, printed by Pynson, have come down to us, for which see Pollard and Redgrave, *Short-Title Catalogue*, entry 18088. While not included in the collected editions of More's *opera*, it was reprinted, in *Epistolarum Philippi Melancthoni libri 4*, London, 1642, where it fills ten folio pages.

man": "Germanus Brixius," says More, "has a forest (*sylva*) and a boat, the glory of the land, the glory of the sea. Would you know what these avail him? Follies ride in the boat, Furies dwell in the wood." As a reply to the Frenchman's charge of faulty versification, More reprints the following line, with the triumphant heading: "Against this hendecasyllable, or rather, verse of thirteen syllables, extracted from the *Antimorus* of Germanus Brixius, Frenchman,"

Exaussisse, hominumque in ora protulisse.

On this More writes two epigrams, the first of which I translate:

Often and for long, in amazement, I have tried to find out how it happens, Brixius, that you make verses so much longer than any ancient or modern poet. But at last I have learned that you are in the habit of measuring your verses not by meter or by feet, but by cubits.

In the meantime, Erasmus was writing to Brixius, to prevent a second reply from that source.[56] He now was successful in conciliating the antagonists; and although they do not appear to have met at Calais, in May or June of 1520,[57] as More had expected they would, they maintained a willingness to meet when opportunity offered. In 1527, Brixius writes to Erasmus[58] that he is looking forward, with cordial pleasure, to seeing More and is hoping to be friends with him. Again, Erasmus wrote to Brixius in 1528, in reply to a letter not extant: "I had not known that More was in

---

[56] Allen, IV, 291; in this letter, dated June 25, 1520, Erasmus does not scruple to warn Brixius that he is hurting himself rather than More; the tone is highly critical.

[57] Preserved Smith, in his *Erasmus* (New York, 1923), p. 93, says that this meeting took place; but I do not find a record of it in the letters to which he refers.

[58] Allen, VII, 58.

Paris. I wish to know what manner of conversation prevailed between you."[59] Thus the two appear to have met; but we must leave the quarrel somewhat inconclusive. Equally so is the "Judgment upon Brixius and More" in four Latin lines by a contemporary, John Leland:

> Brixius est niuei candoris plenus, & ille
> Iudicij veri libera verba serit.
> Brixius aequauit mellito carmine Morum,
> Clarior ingenij nomine Morus erat.[60]

(Brixius is splendidly brilliant, and the other uttered fluent words of sound sense. Brixius has matched More in honeyed song, but More had the greater renown for talent.)

Unsatisfactory as this seems, Leland is right in refusing to discount More's antagonist, who commanded the admiration of Erasmus by his work as scholar and divine, and who as a poet, within the academic conventions, was no worse than scores of others.[61]

Before leaving More's satire, we should notice his "character" of Lalus, the Gallicized Englishman. This poem of about fifty verses, though too long for a right epigram, is exactly such as we shall continually find associated with epigrams. Perhaps it is an example of Scaliger's multiplex or composite epigram, a succession of points upon a single theme. The Frenchified and the Italianate Englishman became, as we know, familiar figures in Elizabethan litera-

---

[59] *Ibid.*, 501.

[60] An account of his *epigrammata*, first published in 1589, is given *infra*, pp. 89-92.

[61] Brixius and his poem which started the controversy are alluded to by Rabelais in the Fourth Book of Pantagruel, Chapter XXI (Motteux's translation): ". . . and have some stately cenotaph to my memory, as Dido had to that of her goodman Sichaeus; . . . Statius to his father; Germain of Brie to Hervé, the Breton tarpaulin."

ture, particularly in satire. In describing Lalus, More uses some form of the word *Gallicus* in almost every line. I quote two passages in translation:

> . . . He keeps
> One only servant.—This man, too, is French;
> And could not, as I think, e'en by the French,
> Be treated more in fashion of the French;
> He clothes him meanly,—that again is French;
> Stints him with meagre victuals,—that is French;
> Works him to death,—and this again is French;
> Belabours him full oft,—and that is French. . . .

> With accent French he speaks the Latin tongue,
> With accent French the tongue of Lombardy,
> To Spanish words he gives an accent French,
> German he speaks with the same accent French.
> In truth, he seems to speak with accent French
> All but the French itself. The French he speaks
> With accent British. . . .[62]

Here also we should record that in common with most non-classical writers[63] More includes a number of versified jests, or *contes*, such as make up the printed jest-books. Although such a mixture of types always scandalizes critics of exacting standards,[64] one has no difficulty in seeing the close relation of the jest to the epigram or in understanding how readers might take no offense at finding them together. Two

[62] From Marsden's incomplete version, *Philomorus*, p. 223.

[63] And some late classical ones; as, in the Greek Anthology, Lucian, Lucilius, and Nicharcus. More's "In Ridiculum Judicium, e Graeco," for example, translates this epigram by Nicharcus (Paton, IV, 188, 189): "A stone-deaf man went to law with another stone-deaf man, and the judge was much deafer than the pair of them. One of them contended that the other owed him five months' rent, and the other said that his opponent had ground corn at night. Says the judge, looking at them: 'Why are you quarreling? She is your mother; you must both maintain her.'"

[64] Such as Ben Jonson; compare also the saying of Boileau, with comment, *supra*, p. 8.

or three times, indeed, as in "Canis in Praesepi, Avarus Homo," More versifies a fable and gives it a specific application. A fable, with its moral, may be said to be related to the moralistic epigram exactly as a jest, with its point, is related to the satirical.

More's sepulchral epigrams are of some interest. In common with other epigrammatists, from Greek to modern times, he does not scruple to violate the rule of *nil nisi bonum*. Satirical epitaphs have ever been a favorite form of wit. More's epitaph upon James V, King of Scotland, who fell at Flodden Field in 1513, while not satirical, is by no means complimentary; it denounces the dead monarch for having broken faith with England, and urges other kings to take warning by his fate. One of the two epitaphs upon Henry Abingdon[65] was written with tongue in cheek. It appears that More had been asked to furnish an epitaph for the tomb of this musician and complied with the request; but his verses did not suit the surviving relatives, who demanded something more musical. So More wrote a second epitaph, with a rhyme in each line. It begins,

Hic jacet Henricus, semper pietatis amicus
Nomen Abyngdon erat, si quis sua nomina quaerat.[66]

This pleased the relatives and was engraved on the tomb. More then wrote a third piece relating the affair and saying that one who preferred the second epitaph to the first should be buried in the same tomb with Abingdon and commemo-

---

[65] He was the earliest known Master of the Children of the Chapel Royal; see *The Old Cheque-Book of the Chapel Royal* (ed. Rimbault; Camden Society, 1872), pp. iv, v.

[66] More evidently took a hint from the inscription upon the tomb of King Henry III in Westminster Abbey, beginning,

Tertius Henricus iacet hic pietatis amicus.

The whole is given by Weever, *Antient Funeral Monuments* (1631), p. 235.

rated by the same inscription. We have seen[67] how Brixius attacked the bad taste of More's riming poem, without fully taking into account the circumstances of its composition.

More's first wife, Jane Colt, died in 1510 and in the same year he married Mrs. Alice Middleton, a widow. At some time within the next few years he composed an ingenious epitaph to be inscribed upon the tomb within which he and his two wives should lie. This epitaph he printed in his *Epigrammata*. At the time of his resigning the Lord Chancellorship, in 1532, he busied himself with erecting a monument in Chelsea Church, and, the remains of his first wife having been brought thither, this verse-epitaph was there inscribed, below a prose epitaph which he had composed for himself. And though his own remains never reached the resting-place he had prepared for them, the verses he wrote constitute an interesting memorial of that strange jocularity which characterized him, even on the headsman's platform. As translated by Wrangham, the epitaph reads thus:

> Within this tomb, Jane, wife of More, reclines:
> This, More for Alice and himself designs.
> The first, dear object of my youthful vow,
> Gave me three daughters and a son to know;
> The next,—ah! virtue in a stepdame rare.
> Nursed my sweet infants with a mother's care.
> With both my years so happily have past,
> Which most my love, I know not—first, or last.
> O! had religion, destiny allow'd
> How smoothly, mix'd, had our three fortunes
>   flow'd.
> But be we in the tomb, in heaven allied:
> So kinder death shall grant, what life denied.[68]

---

[67] *supra*, p. 54; for Campion's use of these poems as an argument against rime, see *infra*, p. 77.

[68] Cayley, *Memoirs*, I, 134; on the same page is another version, made

An interesting personal epigram, which falls into none of the classes I have named, is entitled, "Against Being Transported with Joy Because He Has Escaped Shipwreck." On similar occasions the Greek epigrammatists wrote votive poems to accompany their offerings to the gods. More, as his title indicates, discounts any rejoicing, because, he says, his joy is bound to be short, for there are on land plenty of ways by which his life may soon be brought to an end.

Two other epigrams of special interest are, according to their titles, translations from English songs. We possess few specimens of the English lyrics which were sung during the first decade of the sixteenth century; and with the thought that some reader may be able to find, or to reconstruct, the originals of these songs, I give a prose rendering:

POEM TRANSLATED FROM AN ENGLISH SONG

O sad heart, pitiably plunged in depths of woe,—break! Let thy torment have this end. Show to your mistress your bleeding wounds. That [*i.e.*, life?] is short which separates us two; how long then shall I in sadness weep and mourn? Come, death, grim death, and set me free from such woes.

A JEST UPON A VOW-BREAKING MISTRESS, TRANSLATED FROM AN ENGLISH SONG

Ye gods, what dreams have come to me this night? The whole machine of the world, overturned, fell to ruin; no light remained to the sun or the moon; and the ocean, swelling, spread over all the land. But a greater wonder—lo! a voice seemed to say to me, "Alas! your mistress has broken her plighted word!"[69]

by Cayley. A prose rendering of this epitaph, one of the earliest English translations from More's Latin poems, was printed in the *Workes* of 1557.

[69] The Latin, in six lines each, may be seen in Cayley, *Memoirs*, II, 293.

Non-epigrammatic poems in More's *Epigrammata*, besides some already mentioned, include a delightful verse-epistle to his children, written from Flanders; a long poem advising his friend Candidus concerning the kind of wife to choose; a poem of the kind usually called *elegiae* or *sylvae*, telling of the author's meeting with a lady whom he had loved as a boy, twenty-five years earlier;[70] and another *sylva* addressed to a lady, in which More excuses himself for having been inattentive toward her on a certain occasion.

Three Latin epigrams by our author, not printed in either edition of *Epigrammata*, may be found in his letters.[71] They relate to a double portrait of Erasmus and Peter Giles, sent as a gift to More in 1517. In acknowledging the gift he wrote two short poems, heading one, "The picture speaks," and the other, "More speaks in person." In the first he compared Erasmus and Peter Giles to Castor and Pollux. After sending the verses to Erasmus, More chanced to show a copy of them to a friar, who said that he did wrong in choosing two brothers as a type of friendship. As a result, we find More writing to Erasmus, a month after his former letter:

". . . I could not tolerate this Friar, though there is some truth in what he says; so I followed up his good suggestion with a bad epigram.

---

[70] The letter to his children was translated by W. J. Walter, *Sir Thomas More, a Selection from His Works* (Baltimore, 1841), p. 357; the poem to Candidus and the elegy to his boyhood mistress, by Wrangham, in Cayley, *Memoirs*, I, 264-269. According to Hazlitt, *Collections and Notes* (2d series), p. 405, the poem to Candidus was first printed in 1515 in a re-edition of the jocular work, *De Generibus Ebreosorum*.

[71] Allen, *Erasmi Epistolae*, III, 106-107, 133; translated in Nichols, *Epistles of Erasmus*, III, 92-93, 133. Two other epigrams by More, not reprinted so far as I know, appeared in John Holt's *Lac Puerorum*, a Latin grammar printed by Wynken de Worde about 1510 and by Pynson in 1520.

The warmest friendship to express,
Castor, I said, loved Pollux less.
On this a Friar disputed, whether
Friendship and Brothers matched together.
Why not? said I, can any other
Love a man better than a brother?
The Friar laughed to hear a saying
Such childish ignorance betraying.
Our house is large and full, said he,
More than two hundred Brothers we;
But hang me, if in all you find
A pair of Brothers of one mind."

During the period when More was confined in the Tower (1534-1535), awaiting judgment and execution, he wrote two English stanzas which were called "ballettes" by the collectors of his *Workes*, but which are more truly epigrams. Both are on a subject which recurs in his writings— that of the changes of fortune. One of the epigrams, entitled "Of Davey the Dycer," begins:

Long was I lady Lucke, your serving man
and now have lost agayne all that I gat.

The other, "Lewys the lost Lover," is reminiscent of *Inveni portum, spes et fortuna valete*:

Ey flatering fortune, loke thou neuer so fayre,
Or neuer so plesantly begin to smile
As though thou wouldst my ruin all repayre,
During my life thou shalt me not begile.
Trust shall I to god, to entre in a while,
His hauen of heauen sure and vniforme.
Euer after thy calme, loke I for a storme.

―< VI >―

ABOUT the year 1535 there came from the press of Thomas Berthelet a jest-book with the title, *Tales, and quicke answers*, later reprinted with the longer title which has become more familiar, *Mery Tales, Wittie Questions and Quicke Answeres* (1567).[72] The original compiler of this book was thoroughly familiar with contemporary Neo-Latin writings, drawing his anecdotes from the *Facetiae* of Poggio, the *Fabulae* of Brant, the *Colloquia* and *Apothegmata* of Erasmus, and similar sources. Seven of the jests he appears to have taken from More's *Epigrammata*.[73] As an example of his use of More, we may quote one of the shorter jests, with its source, entire. I have italicized one bit of phrasing which especially suggests direct translation:

OF THE COURTIER THAT BAD THE BOY HOLDE HIS
HORSE. xlii.

A courtier on a tyme that alyghted of his horse at

[72] Reprinted by W. C. Hazlitt in the first volume of *Shakespeare Jest-Books*, 1864, 1881, 1887. In its first form the book contained 114 jests, to which twenty-six were added in 1567. As will be seen, the parallels with More appear in the earlier as well as in the later edition.

[73] Cf. jest 11, "Of him that kissed the mayd with the longe nose," with More's *De Tyndaro* (Cayley, *Memoirs*, II, 325); 41, "Of the Uplandysshe man, that sawe the kynge," with *De rege et rustico* (p. 331); 42, "Of the courtier that bad the boy holde his horse," with *De aulico, ridiculum* (p. 334); 56, "Of hym that at a skyrmyshe defended him with his feet," with *In militem fugacem, et annulatum* (p. 334); 83, "Of the poure man, into whose house theues brake by nyghte," with *In scurram pauperem* (p. 340); 88, "Of hym that had sore eyes," with *De Fusco potore* (p. 330); 89, "Of the olde woman that had sore eyes," with *De chirurgo et anu* (p. 337).

A summary of the sources of *Mery Tales* will be found in Ernst Schulz's *Die Englischen Schwankbücher bis . . . 1607, Palaestra*, 117 (Berlin, 1912), pp. 30-31. For a fuller treatment, see H. de Vocht, "*Mery Tales, Wittie Questions and Quicke Answeres* and their Source," *Anglia*, XXXIII (1910), 120 ff., and A. L. Stiefel, "Die Quellen Der Englischen Schwankbücher des 16. Jahrhunderts," *Anglia*, XXXI (1908), 453 ff. Douglas Bush, "Some Sources for the *Mery Tales, Wittie Questions and Quicke Answeres*," *Modern Philology*, XX (1923), 275, adds some sources in Erasmus's *Adagia*.

an Inde [Inne] gate sayde to a boye that stode therby:
Ho, syr boye, holde my horse. The boye, *as he had ben
aferde*, answered: O maister, this is a fierce horse; is
one able to holde him? Yes, quod the courtier, one
may holde hym well inough. Well, quod the boye, if
one be able inough, than I pray you holde hym your
owne selfe.

DE AULICO, RIDICULUM

Quum descendit equo, de circumstantibus uni
　　Aulicus hunc teneas quisquis es, inquit, equum.
Ille, *ut erat pavidus*, dixit: Domine ergo ferocem
　　Hunc rogo qui teneat, sufficit unus, equum?
Unus ait potis est retinere, subintulit ille:
　　Si potis est unus, tu potes ipse tuum.

Again, More's epigram *De rege et rustico* begins:

　　Rusticus in sylvis nutritus venit in urbem.

The forty-first jest in *Tales, and quicke answers*, which
tells the same story, begins:

　　An vplandysshe man, nourysshed in the woddes,
　　came on a tyme to the citie.

The epigram ends:

　　Hiccine rex? puto me derides, rusticus inquit,
　　　Ille mihi picta veste videtur homo.

And the jest:

　　. . . Is that the kyng, quod the villayne? what, thou
　　mockest me, quod he; me thinke that is a man in a
　　peynted garment.

In some of the other five jests under discussion there is
parallel phrasing of the same sort; in one or two only the
anecdote as a whole, or the point of it, is identical with that
in More. More himself may have translated English origi-

nals which the compiler of the jest-book took over. Certainly most of the jests versified in the *Epigrammata* were current either in Greek, Latin, or English before More used them. Yet the English sources would largely be oral; and the compiler's acquaintance with More's book may be assumed, in view of his proved acquaintance with the works of Erasmus and other contemporaries. These facts, taken with the occasional closeness of phrasing, point to direct use of More as the simplest explanation of the parallels. Through their retelling in *Mery Tales*, some of these jests of More's found a place in later collections.[74] And we shall see that some later compilers also availed themselves of More's *Epigrammata* at first hand.

Verse-translations from More seem to begin with those made by Timothe Kendall, for his *Flowers of Epigrammes* of 1577. Kendall translated twenty-nine, making no distinction between More's own compositions and his translations from the Greek. We shall have more to say later of Kendall's work as translator and anthologist. For the present, we may cite his version of an epigram which was the source, as already noted, of a popular jest:

OF FUSCUS A DRUNKERD

A certaine man in phisicke skild,
  to F. spake in this wise:
F. drinke not ouermuch (take heed)
  for drinke will loose your eyes.
He pausd vppon this sentence giuen,
  and pondered what was spoke:

---

[74] For example, in *Pasquils Iests, mixed with Mother Bunches Merriments* (1604) we find More's *De Tyndaro* retold as "Of a yong Gentleman that would haue kissed a mayd with a long nose" (Hazlitt, *Shakespeare Jest-Books*, III, 41); in *The Pleasant Conceites of Old Hobson* (1607), the thirtieth jest (Hazlitt, III, 45) includes More's anecdote *De Fusco potore*; and the thirteenth and twenty-third jests in the "Certayne Conceyts and Jests" published in *The Philosophers Banquet* (1614, etc.) correspond to More's *De chirurgo et anu* and *In scurram pauperem*.

And when he had bethought hym, thus
at last his mind he broke.
I will by drinkyng loose myne eyes
quoth he, tis better so
Than for to keepe them for the worms
to gnaw them out below.[75]

How much more diffuse is Kendall's English than More's
Latin may be judged from the fact that in the Latin this
epigram is but four lines long.

At about the time Kendall did his work, we may judge,
Sir Nicholas Bacon (1509-1579) amused himself with the
literary exercises which he collected in a manuscript headed,
"The Recreations of his Age."[76] Among the moralistic
poems, hymns, translations, and epigrams of this manuscript are two English versions of epigrams by More.
Bacon's "Of a Fryer and a Marryner" translates at considerable length More's *De nautis ejicientibus monachum in
tempestate*,[77] a jest of sailors who, during a storm, con-
fessed their sins to a friar and then threw him overboard
to lighten the ship of their weight of sin. The other translation we may quote entire, with its original, as showing
that Bacon was able to hold the English to the same length
as the Latin—though he did not do entire justice to the
point of the epigram:

OF JACK AND GYLLE

Of Jacke and Gylle the maryage is as fyne
As of the colde water and the hotte wyne:
Jacke louethe his Gylle as hotte as any fyer,

---

[75] More's *De Fusco potore* (Cayley, *Memoirs*, ii, 330); Kendall's translation will be found in the facsimile reprint of *Flowers of Epigrammes*
made by the Spenser Society, 1874, p. 174.

[76] Printed by Daniel at Oxford, 1903; not issued, however, until 1919.

[77] Cayley, *Memoirs*, II, 321. Bacon's translation is reprinted in *Philomorus*, p. 271.

But Gylle louethe hur Jacke with a watrye desyer:
A match well made, for shoulde bothe alyke burne
Soe mighte their flames their howse to perill turne.[78]

De Phyllide et Prisco, impariter amantibus.
Tam Phyllis cupido bene nubet candida Prisco
    Quam bene spumanti vitrea lympha mero.
Phyllida Priscus amat calido ferventius igne,
    Frigidius gelida Priscus amatur aqua.
Jungetur tuto, nam si simul ardeat illa,
    Sustineat flammas quae domus una duas?

In 1582 Richard Stanyhurst's translation of four books of
the *Aeneid* was printed at Leyden, and in the following
year it was reissued at London. At the end of this work, in
an appendix of "Certayne Poetical Conceites," Stanyhurst
included five translations from More, four of them in his
best "English heroicall Verse."[79] He rarely wrote a better
hexameter than the first in his translation entitled, "Of a
Craking Cvtter, extracted owt of Syr *Thomas Moore* his
Latin Epigrams":

Linckt was in wedlock a loftye Thrasonical huf snuffe.

Yet this translates barely the first two words, *Thrasonis
uxorem*, of the original.[80] More's verse loses all of its concision and most of its point in Stanyhurst's renderings. I
quote the following in full:

~~~~~~~

[78] The point might be rendered thus:
    'Tis safer so: if she matched his desires,
    What house could stand the heat of two such fires?
[79] Reprinted by Sidney H. Atkins, "Certain of Sir Thomas More's Epigrams Translated by Stanihurst," *Modern Language Review*, xxvi (1931),
338.
[80] *Ridiculum, in minacem* (Cayley, ii, 314); a free rendering of the
whole will be found *infra*, p. 72.

HESPERVS HIS CONFESSION,
WRITTEN IN LATIN BY THE SAYD SYR THOMAS MOORE

Hesperus his faulty liuehood too cal toe recounting
Mynding, too be shriuen with woont accustomed hastned.
When that he told playnely, what crym's most sinful he
 practisd,
Yeet thee goastlye father laboring more deepely toe ransack
His formere liuing: by distinct article asked
Eu'rye sin, and naming by peecemeal curius eche fault,
At leingth demaunded, wheather, with sorcerye blinded,
Erst he beleefe yeelded toe the bugs infernal? here aunswerd
Hesperus: holye father, doe ye thinck me soe madly be-
 witched
Too beleue in the deuils? I tel you truelye, toe great payn's
Stil I take enduring, in God yeet scantlye beleeuing.[81]

Stanyhurst reprinted More's riming epitaph upon Henry
Abingdon, and attempted a translation, though with an
apology—fully warranted—for his rimes. It begins,

Here lyeth old *Henry*, no freend to mischeuus *enuye.*
Surnamed *Abyngdon*, to al men most hertelye *welcoom.*
Clerk he was in *wellis*, where tingle a great manye *bellis.*[82]

Besides the epigrams cited, Stanyhurst translated the jest of
the mariners and the friar, previously utilized by Kendall
and Sir Nicholas Bacon; the story of the knight who would
kiss a long-nosed girl, a favorite in the jest-books; and the
humorous recipe for overcoming a strong breath which
Kendall had translated and Harington was to translate
some years later.

 Francis Thynne, the Lancaster herald, who was a dili-
gent antiquary and Chaucerian scholar, appears to have

[81] For the original, see Cayley, II, 345, *De Hespero Confitente*; it is eight
lines in length.
[82] The beginning of More's Latin is quoted *supra*, p. 60.

been the next translator of More. His *Emblemes and Epigrammes*, presented in manuscript to Lord Thomas Egerton in 1600, was largely the work of earlier years and exemplifies that verbosity which prevailed in English verse throughout the 1570's and 1580's. Besides the epigram upon the illiterate bishop already quoted (*supra*, p. 48), Thynne translated two of More's skits upon astrologers and one upon wives, and retold with a slight addition the anecdote of the knight and the long-nosed girl.[83] Nowhere does he make mention of his sources.

When Sir John Harington published his treatise on domestic sanitation, *The Metamorphosis of Ajax* (1596), he felt the need of citing precedents to justify his choice of such a "stale" subject. One of the writers to whom he points as having exemplified freedom in language and theme is Sir Thomas More. He quotes two poems from the *Epigrammata* and gives terse English renderings of them. One of these translations, that of More's recipe for covering up a strong breath by eating onions—and then covering the fumes of onions by eating garlic, and so on—Harington included in the manuscript collection of his epigrams which was published after his death.[84] The other epigram he util-

---

[83] *Emblemes and Epigrames* (Early English Text Society, 1876), pp. 60, 85, 59, 70. Furnivall, in his "Forewords," remarks that the book contains "the wife-worried Thynne's opinions on wives—who're always necessary evils, the best is bad; who're good when they die of old age, better when they die after some time during your life, and best when they die at once." The epigram to which Furnivall refers (his edition, p. 59), however, is a version of this one by More (Cayley, II, 321), who was happily married:

Ad quendam cui uxor mala domi.
Uxor amice tibi est semper mala: quam male tracta
Fit pejor: sed fit pessima, quando bene.
Sed bona si moriatur erit, melior tamen id si
Te faciat vivo: ast optima, si propere.

[84] I, 47; in McClure's edition (1930), No. 48. The passage in *The Metamorphosis of Ajax* here discussed will be found in the Chiswick edition (1814), pp. 38-40.

izes is one of More's renderings from the Greek Anthology.

The next English borrowing from More was that by Samuel Rowlands, a popular and prolific satirist, who included in his *Humors Looking Glasse* (1608) a version of the epigram *Ridiculum, in minacem*. This already had been translated by Kendall, under the title, "The Jest of a Jackbragger," and by Stanyhurst; Rowlands's translation comes from a period of better epigram-writing, and effectively preserves the qualities of the original, though he may have used an English version as his source rather than More's Latin:

> One of these Cuccold-making Queanes
> did graft her husbands head:
> who arm'd with anger, steele and horne
> would kill him stain'd his bed,
> And challeng'd him vnto the field
> Vowing to haue his life,
> Where being met, sirha (quoth he,)
> I doe suspect my Wife
> Is scarce so honest as she should,
> You make of her some vse:
> Indeed said he I loue her well,
> Ile frame no false excuse.
> O! d'ye confesse? by heauens (quoth he)
> Had'st thou deni'de thy guilt,
> This blade had gone into thy guts
> Euen to the verie Hilt.[85]

An interesting illustration of the kinship of jests and epigrams comes from *The Philosophers Banquet* (1614); as

---

[85] Reprint by the Hunterian Club, 1872, p. 8. The point was used by Jonson in *Every Man in His Humor*, III, 2; cf. C. R. Baskerville, *English Elements in Jonson's Early Comedy* (Austin, 1911), p. 116.

the passage in question includes one of the most popular of More's jokes, we quote it in full:[86]

"A certaine conceyted Traueller being at a Banquet, where chanced a flye to fall into his cuppe, which hee (being to drinke) tooke out for himselfe, and afterwards put in againe for his fellow; being demanded his reason, answered, that for his owne part he affected them not, but it might be some other did.

"There is extant to this Ieast, an Epigram of Syr Thomas Moores, which I haue here inserted, as followeth:—

> *Muscas e Cratere tulit Conuiua, priusquam*
> *Ipse bibit: reddit rursus vt ipse bibit;*
> *Addidit et causam; muscas ego non amo, dixit;*
> *Sed tamen e vobis nescio an quis amat.*

> Which I English thus:—
> *Out of his Glasse, one tooke a Flye,*
> *In earnest or in ieast*
> *I cannot tell; but hauing drunke,*
> *Return'd it to the rest.*

> *And for hee would offencelesse seeme,*
> *Hee shewed his reason too:*
> *Although I loue them not my selfe,*
> *It may bee some heere doo.*"[87]

Another jest-book shows how More was a channel by which Greek humor came into England. I quote from *A Banquet of Jests* (5th ed., 1639):

"Upon one that had an exceeding long nose, and great,

---

[86] Reprinted in Hazlitt, *Shakespeare Jest-Books* (1864), III, 15-16. Another translation of the epigram here quoted appeared in *Wits Recreations* (1640, etc.); and John Donne, the younger, includes a version of it in *Donnes Satyr* (1662).

[87] This same English version appears in all editions of John Cotgrave's *Wits Interpreter* (1655) under the title "On a Flye in a glass."

and gag'd teeth, standing some distance one from another,
Sir *Thomas More* made this Epigram:

> *Si tuus in solem statuatur nasus hiante*
> *Ore, bene ostendes dentibus hora quota est.*

Thus Englished.
Gape 'against the Sun, and by thy teeth and nose,
'Tis easie to perceive, how the day goes."

This English couplet was reprinted in *Wits Recreations,*
the most popular seventeenth-century anthology of epigrams. More's Latin, however, translated the Greek of the
Emperor Trajan.[88]

But we cannot hope to trace More through all the jest-
books and collections of epigrams. We should note that Sir
John Mennis and Rev. James Smith, the collectors and editors of *Wits Recreations selected from the Finest Fancies of
Moderne Muses,* included six translations besides the one
just noted.[89] Edward May's *Epigrams Divine and Morall*
(1633) which, as we shall see, leans heavily on Kendall's
Flowers of Epigrammes, contains some secondhand paraphrases of epigrams by More. John Donne, the younger,
translated some twenty-five of More's poems and included
his translations in *Donnes Satyr* of 1662, with no mention of
their source. The most considerable translator of More in
the seventeenth century (and perhaps in any century) was
Thomas Pecke, who printed forty renderings, referred to
on the title page as "the most select in Sir Thom. More," in

[88] Paton, IV, p. 272.

[89] In the reprint of 1874 (Hotten's), Nos. 85, 86, 254, 278, 283, 287,
translate More's *De Fusco potore* (330), *Ad Sabinum* (336), *Ridiculum, in
ministrum* (306), *Aliud, in astrologum uxoris impudicae maritum* (288),
In Scurram pauperem (340), *De Phyllide et Prisco, impariter amantibus*
(344). (Numbers in parentheses refer to Cayley, *Memoirs,* Vol. II.) Epigram
No. 571, "On Gut," in *Wits Recreations* imitates More's *In Pinguem quendam patrem* (349). No. 283, here listed as from More, goes back to the
Greek Anthology.

his *Parnassi Puerperium* of 1659. One of Pecke's versions has been quoted (*supra*, p. 43). Charles Cotton Englished three of More's epigrams for his *Poems on Several Occasions* (1689). The several eighteenth-century anthologies of English epigrams all contain translations from More. In the nineteenth century a few translations by Archdeacon Francis Wrangham and by Arthur Cayley appeared in Cayley's *Memoirs of Sir Thomas More* (1808), and a larger number, made by John Marsden, in *Philomorus* (1878) and *Fasciculus* (1869). An American admirer of More, W. J. Walter, translated some of the longer poems from the *Epigrammata* for his volume, *Sir Thomas More, a Selection from His Works* (Baltimore, 1841). It is a little unfortunate that in Francis Pierrepont Barnard's *A Fardel of Epigrams*, which is almost the sole collection of English renderings from epigram-writers of the Renaissance, More is represented only by a poem which versifies a jest told in one of his English prose works.

We may consider briefly some of the Continental echoes of More's *Epigrammata*. The publication and reprintings of the entire volume have been noted already, as well as the copious selections in Duchesne's *Flores Epigrammatum* (1555). Other miscellanies, such as *Mensa Philosophica* (1602) and *Jocorum atque Seriorum* (1604), reprinted a few of the best epigrams.[90] The earliest rendering into the German vernacular seems to be that in George Rodolphe Weckerlin's *Gaistliche und Weltliche Gedichte* (Amsterdam, 1641), but others appeared throughout the seven-

---

[90] In the Leipzig (1603) edition of *Mensa Philosophica*, More's epigram of the astrologer with the unfaithful wife appears at p. 306; that on getting rid of a bad breath at p. 385; on the monk thrown overboard by the sailors at p. 442; on the fly in the drinking-glass at p. 477; others at pp. 312, 390, 391, 455.

In *Jocorum atque Seriorum* (Liege, 1604-05; Frankfort, 1617) the epigram upon the illiterate bishop appears at I, 136; on the monk thrown overboard, at III, 197; on Sabinus, the cuckold, at I, 42.

teenth century.[91] The greatest German admirer of the *Epigrammata* was J. B. Menke, who included a translation in his *Galante Gedichte* of 1705, and several others, with a commendation of More's work, in his *Schertzhoffte Gedichte* of the following year. A translation of More's epigram upon Sabinus, the cuckold, into Dutch, apparently to be dated *c.* 1640, will be found in Sloane MS. 2764 (fol. 114).

The good repute of More's epigrams among his own countrymen, for a century or more after his death, is established by evidence more direct than the making of translations. John Leland, the antiquary, who was a late contemporary of More's, thus referred to him in some verses "Concerning certain poets of our time":

> Ætas nostra sales, ac *Mori* laudat acumen,
> Gratior haec eadem posteritasque canet.[92]

> (Our age lauds the wit and acumen of More; even more gratefully may posterity hymn these excellences.)

Leland's highest praise of More, however, is embodied in his epigram *Ad Valerium Martialem*. Here, after four lines in which he admits that Martial is most witty of all the famous and learned poets who have written epigrams, he introduces More with the comment that with as good material to work on as Martial had, More might have equalled him. Leland then praises More's easy wit and calls upon Martial to divide honors with him. Fifty years after Leland wrote, Gabriel Harvey was jotting in his books occasional notes expressing his admiration for More. Among "the fine poesies of Sir Thomas More," he singled out for praise "his Latin Epitaph upon his two wives, Joane, &

---

[91] See Gilbert Waterhouse, *The Literary Relations of England and Germany in the Seventeenth Century* (Cambridge, 1914), pp. 17, 60.

[92] *Principum ac illustrium . . . encomia*, 1589, p. 22.

Alice."[93] Harvey drew upon the *Epigrammata* to make a point in *The Trimming of Thomas Nashe* (1597), when he wrote:

". . . as wofull as the Cunny which escaping the Weasell fell into the hunters net, of which was that fugitive Epigram, Would to God the Weasell with my blood had sucked out my life, for now I am kept a pray for ravening dogs."

This is virtually a translation from More.[94] Another interesting allusion is made by Thomas Campion, who, in his *Observations in the Art of English Poesie* (1602), cites More as an opponent of rime:

"For the establishing of this argument, what better confirmation can be had than that of Sir Thomas Moore in his booke of Epigrams, where he makes two sundry Epitaphs vpon the death of a singing-man at Westminster, the one in learned numbers and dislik't, the other in rude rime and highly extold: so that he concludes, *tales lactucas talia labia petunt*, like lips like lettuce."

Samuel Daniel, in his reply to Campion, does not allude specifically to this passage, but he mentions More as "a great ornament to this land, and a Rymer,"—as indeed he was, in his English poems. William Vaughan, in *The Golden Grove* (1600), mentions "Sir Thomas Moore . . . whose poeticall works are as yet in great regard." But the best Jacobean estimate of More's epigrams is that of Henry Peacham in *The Compleat Gentleman* (1622, 1634); in a passage which refers to a number of epigrams we have already noticed, Peacham shows himself to have been a delighted and discriminating reader:

"In the daies of Henry the 8. . . . flourished Sir Thomas

[93] *Gabriel Harvey's Marginalia*, collected and edited by G. C. Moore Smith (Stratford-upon-Avon, 1923), p. 234.
[94] *Cunicula loquitur, quae elapsa mustelae incidit in disposita venatorum retia*, in Cayley, II, 283.

Moore, sometime Lord Chancellor of England: a man of most rich and pleasant invention: his verse fluent, nothing harsh, constrained or obscure, wholly composed of conceipt, and inoffensive mirth, that he seemeth *ad lepores fuisse natum*. How wittily doth he play upon the Arch-cuckold Sabinus, scoff at Frenchified Lalus, and Hervey a French cowardly Captaine, beaten at sea by our English, and his shippe burned, yet his victory and valor, to the English disgrace, proclaimed by Brixius a Germane Pot-aster? What can be more loftie than his gratulatory verse to King Henry upon his Coronation day, more wittie than that Epigramme upon the name of Nicolaus an ignorant Physitian, that had been the death of thousands, and Abyngdons Epitaph? More sweet than that nectar Epistle of his, to his daughters Margaret, Elizabeth, and Cicely? But as these ingenious exercises bewrayed in him an extraordinary quickness of wit and learning, so his Utopia his depth of judgment in State affairs. . . . In his yonger yeeres, there was ever a friendly and virtuous emulation, for the palme of invention and poesie, betweene William Lillie the Author of our Grammar, and him, as appeareth by their several translations of many Greek Epigrammes, and their invention tried upon one subject; notwithstanding they lov'd and liv'd together as dearest friends."[95]

Before taking our leave of More, let us summarize. We have found an author putting forth a book of epigrams in which translations and imitations, often without acknowledgement of sources, are mingled with original compositions; in which versified jests and fables stand as epigrams; and in which odes, a verse-epistle, "society verse," and occasional verse also find a place. We have seen that his epi-

---

[95] *The Compleat Gentleman* (reprinted, Oxford, 1906), pp. 92-93. Peacham mistakenly refers to Brixius as "Germane"; he was probably misled by his Latinate given name, Germanus.

grams range from moralistic truisms to keen personal satire, and include commendatory and sepulchral pieces, both serious and satirical; and that in length they vary from two lines to fifty lines. We have seen how some of his compositions were circulated in manuscript and known to his friends before they were printed; and how a few stinging verses gave rise to a considerable literary controversy. Finally we have seen his work reprinted, translated, and included, often with no acknowledgement to him, in later collections, with a few of his pieces becoming especially popular and appearing many times. In all this, More is fairly typical of the epigrammatists of our period. In knowing him, we go far toward understanding the epigram-literature of the following one hundred and fifty years.

I nunc Pegaseo gradu Camaena,
Et docti pete tecta Martialis.
Scis tu certo ubi sint? viamque nosti?[1]

—JOHN LELAND

CHAPTER III · SCHOLARLY EPIGRAMMATISTS
AFTER MORE

MANY Englishmen besides More wrote and published Latin epigrams in the sixteenth century. This chapter considers the work of a few of them, carrying the story down to Thomas Campion, whose *Poemata* of 1595 is reserved for treatment in a later chapter.

As we have seen, literary conventions demanded that a man of learning should produce epigrams, whether merely to display his wit or to pay a tribute to a new book, a noble patron, or a great man recently dead. The passing of a nobleman, a scholar, or a churchman was the occasion of an outburst of sepulchral verses by all of the surviving *literati*, each of whom might rest secure in the hope that he, in his turn, would some day be the subject of similar tributes. Thus Milton, in *Lycidas*:

> So may some gentle muse
> With lucky words favor my destined urn.
> And as he passes, turn,
> And bid fair peace be to my sable shroud!

"Whenever some celebrated person dies," says Ménage, the great seventeenth-century French scholar, "I am accustomed to remark: 'He will not pass *unepitaphed*.'"[2] The fashion

---

[1] "Go now, O Muse, with the pace of Pegasus, and seek the dwelling-place of the learned Martial. Do you know for sure where it is? Do you know the way?" These lines form the opening of Leland's epigram, *Ad Camaenam, vt Martialem salutet*, probably written *c.* 1540, published in *Principium ac illustrium, etc.* (1589), p. 8.

[2] *Ménagiana* (Amsterdam, 1693), I, 99; here translated.

thus alluded to had been followed throughout the period of the Renaissance, whether on the continent or in England. And with equal assurance it might have been predicted of a new book, It will not appear uncommended; for most books of our period were ushered into the world with a salvo of laudatory epigrams by friends of the author, usually printed at the beginning of the volume. Thus a man with any smack of letters or with any freehold in the learned world is likely to be represented somewhere, either in printed books or in manuscripts, by at least a few epigrams.

We have already noticed the *Progymnasmata*, or exercises in translation, of William Lily, More's friend and John Colet's choice as first headmaster of St. Paul's School. Aside from these, the greater part of Lily's epigram-writing grew out of a *bellum grammaticale* which centered upon the figure of Robert Whittington, a rival writer of Latin grammars. This worthy in 1513 petitioned the regents of Oxford University for the laureateship, that is, for the style of *laureatus*, bestowed with a ceremonial crowning with laurel and carrying with it the doctorate in poetry and rhetoric. After receiving this honor, Whittington signed himself, in several of his works, *Protovates Angliae* (chief poet of England), a title resented by his fellow-grammarians, William Lily and William Horman. Strangely enough, John Skelton, who for some years had been *laureatus* and held a better claim to the title of *Protovates*, seems to have been on Whittington's side in the ensuing controversy. Either before or after Lily and Horman had attacked him, Whittington uttered strictures upon the grammatical writings of Horman, and there is some evidence that he posted on the door of St. Paul's verses attacking Lily.

As a nickname for Whittington, his opponents adopted *Bossus*, a term borrowed from the English name, "the Bosse," given to a fountain at Billingsgate. It is a modern conjecture that, since this fountain had been erected by

Richard Whittington, the famous Lord Mayor, identity of surnames was the ground for connecting the grammarian and the fountain.[3] Perhaps the real explanation would be clearer if we knew the personal appearance and manners of Robert Whittington. The part of the fountain which delivered the water had the form of a bear; and the bear also became a symbol for Lily's and Horman's opponent. In the books written by these men and their friends against "the chief poet of England,"[4] there was printed at several places a picture, of obvious import, showing a bear attacked by six dogs. The name *Bossus* also allowed of division into the terms *bos* (ox) and *sus* (pig), suggesting further witticisms against its bearer.

At least three printed books resulted from this rather puerile controversy. The first is Lily's *Antibossicon* (1521), in three parts: the first titled merely *Antibossicon*; the second, *In aenigmata Bossi Antibossicon secundum. Ad Guil. Hormanum*; and the third, *Antibossicon tertium. Ad Guil.*

---

[3] Some lines in the extant poems allow of the interpretation that Whittington himself had adopted the name *Bossus*, doubtless with no reference to the fountain; this connection, then, rather than the invention of the nickname, would be the contribution of Lily and Horman.

[4] Whittington's Latin poetry may best be seen in his *Opusculum* printed by Wynken de Worde in 1519. This contains panegyrics and laudatory epigrams to Henry VIII, Cardinal Wolsey, Sir Thomas More, Charles Brandon, and John Skelton "of Louvain, poet" (Skelton had been made *laureatus* by the University of Louvain). One of the epigrams is an hexastichon introducing half a dozen puns upon the name of More. This volume is not listed in the *Short-Title Catalogue*; but a copy in Heber's collection is fully described, with copious quotations, by Dibdin, *Typographical Antiquities* (1812), II, 181-182.

In the same volume of Dibdin many other specimens of Whittington's epigrams are reprinted (pp. 178-202) from his various grammatical works. Nearly all of these are invectives against his critics, especially against his arch-critic, Zoilus, who may be presumed to be William Horman. *Humiliabit calumniatorem* (He will bring low the slanderer) is a favorite expression of Whittington's. Other specimens of his Latin verse were printed for purposes of attack in Lily's and Horman's books, mentioned below in the text.

Hormanum. The whole was printed as the second section in Lily's *Epigrammata* (1521), the first section comprising epigrams not having to do with Whittington.[5] The second volume, printed in the same year, carried the title *Antibossicon Guil. Hormani ad Guilelmum Lilium*. This contains, among other material not written by Horman, a verse-epistle by Robert Aldrich, another celebrated grammarian of the time, and an attack by Whittington against Horman, printed to furnish material for reply. The third volume was Whittington's *Epistola respons. ad G. Hormani Invectivas & Dialogus cum eodem* (1521).[6] Aside from furnishing specimens of academic invective and demonstrating the lengths to which *odium scholasticum* may carry one, the compositions in these volumes possess little importance. The circumstances of the controversy are more interesting than the attacks and counterattacks themselves.

It is unfortunate that Lily's short collection entitled *Epigrammata* is no longer available. Some of its contents, however, are to be found in Harl. Ms. 540,[7] copied in the handwriting of John Stow. One poem is an epitaph upon the author's wife, Agnes Lily; another has as its subject the pictures of Erasmus and Peter Giles which More had received and upon which he, too, wrote some verses; two epigrams are addresses to Polydore Vergil. Most interesting of all is a retort upon John Skelton, "who slandered his

---

[5] These bibliographical details are here set down because previous accounts have confused these titles. No copy of the first section, the *Epigrammata*, seems to be extant, as only the *Antibossicon* is listed in the *Short-Title Catalogue* (entry 15606). But the volume with all its four parts was in the library at Lambeth Palace in 1843, and was described in detail by S. R. Maitland in his *List of Early Printed Books* (1843), pp. 415-416.

[6] Not in *Short-Title Catalogue*; for a description, see Dibdin, *Typographical Antiquities* (1812), II, 483, and references there given.

[7] fols. 57v-59r. One of the epigrams here, *De rege castelle Philippo naviganti in hispaniam*, is cited by Maitland (*op. cit.*, p. 415) from the printed *Epigrammata*.

[*i.e.*, Lily's] poems." This fragment from a forgotten literary controversy (a by-product, perhaps, of the controversy
with Whittington) was reprinted by John Weever in his
Antient Funeral Monuments (1631) and again by Thomas
Fuller. Omitting the Latin, I give Fuller's English rendering:

> With face so bold, and teeth so sharp
> Of viper's venom, why dost carp?
> Why are my verses by thee weigh'd
> In a false scale?—May truth be said?
> Whilst thou, to get the more esteem,
> A learned poet fain wouldst seem:
> Skelton, thou art, let all men know it,
> Neither learned, nor a poet.[8]

Some of Lily's verses, through being included in the Latin
grammar usually called his, have received as wide a circulation and reading, perhaps, as those of any Neo-Latin poet
of his century. On the title page of some early editions of
the *Grammatica Latina*, for example, this quatrain was
printed:

G. LILY EPIGRAMMA

> Pocula si linguae cupias gustare latinae,
> Quale tibi monstret, ecce Coletus iter.
> Non per caucaseos montes aut summa pyrenes
> Te ista per Hybleos sed via ducit agros.[9]

(If you desire to taste the founts of the Latin
tongue, behold the way as Colet shows it to you.
Not over Caucasian mountains or the steeps of the
Pyrenees, but through Hyblean fields does the road
lead you.)

~~~~~~~~~

[8] *Worthies*, ed. Nuttall (London, 1840), II, 462.
[9] *Shakespeare Jahrbuch*, XLIV (1908), 65.

Another poem by Lily, not an epigram, was his *Carmen ad discipulos, de moribus*, placed at the end of the Latin grammar. Quotations from this guide to good schoolboy manners occur several times in the literature of the sixteenth and seventeenth centuries.[10] In 1522, the last year of his life, Lily wrote a panegyric to the Emperor Charles V, upon the occasion of his visit to England.

Considering this grammarian's interest in the writing of Latin verses, together with the fact that such exercises formed an important part of the school discipline of the time, we are not surprised to find that the next two authors to be considered were at one time pupils of Lily at St. Paul's. The first of these is John Constable, who gained much reputation as a Latin poet and rhetorician at Oxford, where he took his first degree in 1511 and his second in 1515. Constable's epigrams were printed by Richard Pynson in 1520, forming a book of sixteen leaves in quarto. A unique copy, that of Robert Burton, the anatomist of melancholy, rests in the Bodleian library.[11] It opens with a prose address to honest readers, in which the author defends the practice of writing trifles and light verses as a recreation when tired with other studies; not all of the verses, he points out, are light. The collection contains a number of moralistic couplets (*De beneficientia, Cognosce teipsum*, etc.), a few satirical epigrams (*In loquacem, De iurisperito*

---

[10] Listed in *Shakespeare Jahrbuch*, XLV (1909), 75 ff. A translation of this poem by John Penkethman, a schoolmaster of the following century, was published in that author's *Onomatophylacium* (1626); printed on one side only of four leaves, so that these leaves could be cut out and pasted into a school-boy's copy of the Latin grammar.

Speaking of Lily's Latin, Foster Watson says: "It is difficult to realize that formerly these verses were probably as well known in England as any lines of the classics." (*English Grammar Schools to 1660* [Cambridge, 1908], p. 107.)

[11] A fragment of another copy has been found; see *Notes and Queries*, 8th ser., x (1896), 289.

iniquo, Ad monachum), a tribute to Oxford men, one to Beam Hall (where he resided), and a considerable number of poems praising William Lily, Sir Thomas More, Bishop Latimer, the King and Queen, and others. Constable also printed a poem on the ages of man, twelve lines in length, devoting two lines to each of six ages. The ending of his epigram *Ad Monachum* reveals an acquaintance with Martial: Constable's *Magnus dicetur verius ardelio* echoes Martial's *magnus es ardelio* (ii, 7). We should note also that this pupil of Lily's joined the hue and cry against Whittington, with an epigram *In Bossum Liliomastigem* (Against *Bossus*, the whipper of Lily), in which he says that *Bossus* has been silenced and now denies the authorship of his own verses. But Constable had not the gift of epigram, and one must agree with the judgment of C. Trice Martin (in the *Dictionary of National Biography*) that his epigrams are "dull and pointless, though the versification is correct."

A more familiar name is that of John Leland, the antiquarian, another pupil of Lily's. He is credited by the *New English Dictionary* with the first use of the English word "epigram"; the date is 1538.[12] Leland appears, however, to have written no epigrams in English. He found time to produce considerable Latin verse, as, for example, a congratulatory ode upon the coronation of Anne Boleyn, and *Laudatio Pacis* (1546), a poem of three hundred and ten lines. A more interesting work is his *Naeniae in mortem Thomae Viati equitis incomparabilis* (1542), a series of about thirty epigrams celebrating the life and death of Sir Thomas Wyatt. This book, dedicated to the Earl of Surrey, shows a lively appreciation of Wyatt as a writer and ex-

---

[12] Sir Thomas Wyatt uses the word in his translation of Plutarch's "Quiet of Mind," written in 1527 and published in 1528; the unique copy of this book, now in the Huntington Library, was not available to the compilers of *N. E. D.*

presses sincere esteem and personal affection for him as a man. "The English tongue has been a formless harmony, without renown," says Leland in one distich; "now it acknowledges your file, learned Wyatt." Again: "Jove's eagle seeks the mountain-tops and tries his strength upon the steeps; such, by nature's dower, was Wyatt." An epigram upon Holbein's portrait says: "Holbein, greatest in the fair art of painting, has drawn Wyatt's image with nicety, but no Apelles portrays his happy qualities and spirit." One epigram takes for its subject Wyatt's ring, another praises his translation from the *Psalms*, another describes his handsome face and figure. Let me reprint, with Fuller's somewhat awkward translation, a quatrain which suggests that Englishmen were consciously thinking of England as a literary rival to Italy:

ANGLUS PAR ITALIS

Bella suum merito jactet florentia Dantem
  Regia Petrarchae carmina Roma probet.
His non inferior patrio sermone Viatus
  Eloquii secum qui decus omne tulit.

("Let Florence fair her Dante's justly boast,
  And royal Rome her Petrarch's numbered feet:
In English Wiat both of them doth coast,
  In whom all graceful eloquence doth meet.")[13]

As a New Year's gift to Henry VIII, in 1546 Leland presented an address telling of his journey and search among the monasteries and colleges of England. This account was published in 1549, with copious additions and comments by John Bale, under the title, *The Laboryouse Journey & Serche of John Leylande, for Englandes Antiquities*.[14] At

---

[13] Fuller's *Worthies* (ed. by Nuttall, 1840), II, 152. The *Naeniae* may be seen in full in Hearne's edition (Oxford, 1770) of Leland's *Itinerary*, or in Miss Foxwell's edition of Wyatt's poems (1913), II, 231 ff.

[14] Reprinted, ed. W. A. Copinger (Manchester, 1895).

the end Bale printed a few of Leland's verses, prefaced by this note:

"As I had fynyshed this present Treatyse, a frind of Johan Leylande brought me these verses of hys, to emprint them with the worke, leaste any thing shulde perysh that came from hym. And I was as glad to perfourme it, as he was to desyre it. I would I myghte so wele geue unto my readers the most noble worke of his Epigrammes, as these fewe verses folowynge."

Bale did not live to see his wish fulfilled. Leland's collected Latin epigrams were not printed until 1589, when they were put through the press by Thomas Newton, together with a collection of Newton's own. Leland's are for the most part laudatory, as indicated by the title, *Principum, ac Illustrium Aliquot & Eruditorum in Anglia Virorum, Encomia, Trophaea, Genethliaca & Epithalamia.* Yet among the two hundred and sixty-five poems included, there is the variety usual in such collections. In length the poems range from one line to seventy-eight, though by far the greater number keep within ten lines. There are two translations from Greek epigrams; and the *in Anglia* of the title is contradicted by tributes to Martial and Catullus. Those addressed to Nicholas Bourbon and Luis Vives were doubtless written when those men actually were in England. For the most part, Leland's titles give us a roll of celebrated English scholars and authors down to the time when he was writing.[15] We have already noticed (pp. 58, 76) the

---

[15] Besides those mentioned in the text, and besides men who were honored for their rank or service to the state rather than for their letters or scholarship, the following receive tributes from Leland: Robert Aldrich, or Aldridge, Roger Ascham, John Barret (probably he who died in 1563), John Bekinsau, Thomas Caius, or Key, William Cecil (perhaps the earliest of tributes to him), John Cheke, John Claymond, John Clement (tutor of More's children), John Clerk (tutor of the Earl of Surrey), Henry Cole, John Colet, Sir Anthony Cooke, Leonard Cox, Thomas Cranmer, George Day, Sir Anthony Denney (who had been a schoolmate of Leland's at

epigram upon Brixius and More and the one comparing More with Martial. Leland also praises the learned daughters of More. Two epigrams pay tribute to a schoolboy, Christopher Smith, who, though scarcely past his tenth year, speaks Latin well and as an actor wins applause in comedy or brings tears by the pathetic quality of his voice in tragedy. There are some personal poems, such as the one on a friend's return, one on the author's studies, and one on his birthday. Several of the epigrams were commendations for books. And there are the usual admonitory or moralistic epigrams, such as *Ad Famam, Applausus Posteritatis*, and *Fama virtutis aeterna*. One, *In Richardum Crokum, calumniatorem*, is a bit of vituperation upon the distinguished Greek scholar who was the first Public Orator of Cambridge University. It is likely that Leland's quarrel grew out of Croke's opposition, in 1529, to the public honors paid Bishop Fisher for his benefactions to St. John's College. The seventeenth-century historian of St. John's speaks of Croke, in this connection, as 'an ambitious, envious, and discontented wretch who had been preferred by him [Fisher] and had eat his bread, and yet had the impudence to charge him with setting up for founder.'[16]

St. Paul's), Sir Thomas Eliot, Erasmus (two epigrams), George Ferrers, Edward Fox, Walter Haddon, Thomas Linacre (four epigrams), Thomas Lupset (three), Sir Richard Morison, Richard Pace, Francis Poins, John Poynet, John Redman, Sir Richard Shelley, John Shepreve, Thomas Smith, Thomas Sulmo, or Some, Robert Talbot, Cuthbert Tunstall, John Twyne, Nicholas Udall (three), Peter Vannes, Polydore Vergil, Nicholas Wilson, Thomas Wriothesley (the one that died in 1534?), and Sir Thomas Wyatt. (This list includes, Erasmus apart, only men whose lives are recorded in *D. N. B.* There are also tributes to men now unknown.) It is possible, also, that the epigram to Edmund Bouer (so spelled both in title and text) was really addressed to Edmund Boner, or Bonner, who later became, as persecuting bishop, the object of much hatred. There is also a tribute to Charles, or Carolo, Cappello, "Venetian orator."

[16] Thomas Baker, *History of St. John's College*, ed. J. E. B. Mayor (Cambridge, 1869), I, 97.

Another epigram attacks Hector Boethius's history of Scotland (1527), saying: 'Dear reader, if you wish me to enumerate the lies that Hector wrote in his history, you should command me also to count the waves of the sea and to number the stars in the clear sky.' It is more pleasant to turn to Leland's praises of Chaucer. One of the three tributes to the poet runs as follows:

DE GALLOFRIDO CHAUCERO, EQUITE

Praedicat Aligerum merito Florentia Dantem,
  Italia & numeros tota (Petrarcha) tuos:
Anglia Chaucerum veneratur nostra poetam,
  Cui Veneres debet patria lingua suas.

(Florence with justice boasts of Dante Alighieri, and all Italy of your numbers, O Petrarch: our England venerates the poet Chaucer, to whom our native tongue owes its graces.)

Another epigram which reveals Leland's genuine enthusiasm for the Revival of Learning, and which celebrates his teacher Lily and other of the earliest English students of Greek authors, should be quoted entire:

INSTAURATIO BONARUM LITERARUM

Ecce renascentis doctrinæ gloria floret,
  Linguarum floret cognitioque trium.
Migrat in Italiam Græcus thesaurus, & artes
  Se reparaturum prædicat usque bonas.
Excolit eloquij viuos Hispania fontes,
  Gallia nunc studijs tota dicata nitet.
Nutrit honorifice doctos Germania multos,
  Quorum sunt orbi nomina nota probe.
Ingeniorum altrix & nostra Britannia, Phræum,
  Tiptotum Viduum, Flaminiumque tulit.
Lumina doctrinae, Grocinus deinde secutus,

Sellingus, Linacer, Latimarusque pius,
Dunstallus, Phænix, Stocleius at*que* Coletus,
Lilius & Paceus, festa corona virum.

Leland's poems, published as they were at a time when
their contemporaneous interest had passed away, attracted
little attention. Thomas Nashe, writing his preface to
Greene's *Menaphon* in the very year of Newton's resur-
rection of Leland, mentions among the few worthy poets of
the age "Thos. Newton with his Leyland." And Meres, in
Palladis Tamia (1598) includes among Englishmen who
were Latin poets "Thomas Newton with his Leyland,"
probably without having read any farther than Nashe's
preface. John Weever quotes the "learned epigram" on
More's daughters, as well as two or three other pieces by
Leland, in his *Antient Funeral Monuments* (1631); but
one passage indicates that Weever was not aware that these
poems had been printed but was using a manuscript of
them. As is fitting, Leland's work has had the greatest interest for antiquarians, and a generation later than Weever,
we find, Thomas Fuller and Anthony à Wood were thoroughly conversant with it. The years covered by the composition of the epigrams appear to be those from about
1530, or a little earlier, to the accession of Edward VI in
1547; and a student of English letters in that period would
do well to acquaint himself with Leland's collection.

$\prec$ II $\succ$

EXCEPT More, the most important and accomplished English author of Latin epigrams in his century was John
Parkhurst, a genial and urbane churchman who was Bishop
of Norwich from 1560 until his death in 1575. His epigrams
were written, for the most part, in the reigns of Henry and
Edward, but no complete edition of them appeared until
1573. Parkhurst had been a brilliant and popular student at

Oxford, proceeding to the bachelor's degree in 1528 and the master's in 1532. For a time he was a tutor at Merton College, where his favorite student was John Jewel. When, fifteen years later, Jewel became a Lecturer in Rhetoric at Corpus Christi College, Parkhurst came from his parish at Cleve to listen to his former pupil and wrote this distich for the occasion:

> Olim discipulus mihi, chare Juelli, fuisti.
> Nunc ero discipulus, te renuente, tuus.

> ("Dear Jewel, scholar once thou wast to me,
> Now 'gainst thy will I scholar turn to thee.")[17]

At about this same time, in 1551, the two young sons of Charles Brandon, Duke of Suffolk, both died within a few hours from attacks of the sweating-sickness. Dr. Thomas Wilson, author of the *Logike* and the *Rhetorique*, had been the boys' tutor, and John Parkhurst had been their father's chaplain. These, with other scholars and divines, by way of consolation to the bereaved Duke prepared a large volume of tributes and elegies, *Vita et Obitus Fratrum Suffolciensium* (1551). The second part of this volume consists of *Epigrammata Varia*, a collection of laudatory and sepulchral epigrams in Latin and in Greek, written by no fewer than eighteen Cambridge men (including Cheke, Haddon, and Wilson) and fifteen Oxford men. Parkhurst appears among the representatives of Oxford, with three poems. A supplement to the volume consists of poems, mainly epitaphs, upon other noble and royal persons; in this section appear five more of Parkhurst's compositions.

Within a year after the accession of Mary, Parkhurst fled from England and took refuge at Zürich, where he made a number of warm friends. During his last years in England he had been urged by friends to publish the collection of

---

[17] Translation by Fuller, *Worthies*, ed. Nuttall (1840), III, 208.

epigrams to which he had been adding ever since his University days. In Zürich he evidently prepared the manuscript for publication, for the prefatory address finally printed is dated from that city in the year 1558.[18] But the accession of Elizabeth brought a change in all his plans, and in 1559 he returned to England with the expectation of a bishopric. As he was on his way back, Fuller tells us,[19] he "was robbed of that little he had, by some searchers appointed for that purpose. Were not these thieves themselves robbed, I mean of their expectation, who hoped to enrich themselves by pillaging an exile and a poet? It grieved him most of all that he lost the fair copy of his Epigrams, though afterwards with much ado he recovered them from his foul papers." When finally ensconced in the bishop's palace 'at Norwich he began to get from his Zürich friends expressions of hope that he would now publish his epigrams. To one of them he wrote: "You recommend me to publish my Epigrams: why should I publish frivolous trifles of this sort? They are certainly contending in some corner of my study with moths and beetles."[20] Copious selections, however, from his religious verses were printed in the widely circulated and often reprinted *Preces Privatae* (1564), a devotional manual having official authority. Finally Parkhurst

---

[18] In the meanwhile some of the serious and religious epigrams had been printed, according to Wood (*Athenae Oxoniensis*, I, 135), at the end of John Shefery's *Summa & Synopsis Novi Testamenti* (Strasburg, 1556), which Parkhurst saw through the press, its author having died in 1542. This fact must account for the book, *Epigrammata Seria* (London, 1560), attributed to Parkhurst by Warton and others, following Wood. Parkhurst's epigrams in Shefery's volume may have had a half-title of this sort, and there may have been an English edition of the whole (or a separate printing of the supplement of epigrams) in 1560. However, I have seen no edition of Shefery's *Summa* and cannot speak with certainty.

[19] *Worthies*, III, 209.

[20] Undated letter to John Wolfius in *Zürich Letters*, edited by Robinson for the Parker Society (Cambridge, 1842), I, 49; Parkhurst's Latin is at p. 28 of the Appendix.

made another fair copy of all his poems, bound them into a manuscript volume, and presented this as a New Year's gift, in 1573, to his old friend, Dr. Thomas Wilson. Wilson saw to it that the volume was printed; the title was *Ioannis Parkhursti Ludicra sive Epigrammata Juvenilia*. Its author was now sixty-one years of age, a grave bishop of an important diocese, urged from time to time, by the Archbishop of Canterbury, to be more rigorous against his Puritan pastors; and this was, and remained, his sole published book.

It made an attractive volume, as printed by John Day in quarto, beginning with complimentary stanzas by Thomas Wilson, Lawrence Humphrey, Bartholomew Traheron, and several others. Then comes a long prose address *Ad Lectorem*,[21] in which Parkhurst makes the usual apologies for thus coming before the world, shows his acquaintance with the Latin epigrams of Sir Thomas More and the English ones of Heywood and Crowley, and answers, in anticipation, the various criticisms which he knows will be passed upon his book. In spite of his title and his continual allusions to his poems as trivial and facetious, we should not forget that a fair share of his collection consists of religious poems which already had been printed in theological or devotional volumes, and of commendations or epitaphs upon noble and royal persons. For the captious he wrote an additional *Admonitio ad Lectorem*, dealing with matters of metre. He defends his frequent use of iambic metres by quoting examples of similar use by Martial and by Nicholas Bourbon; he has treated the first syllable of *chiragra* as short, but so, he says, did Martial, Persius, and Horace; "I make the first syllable of *capone* long—Martial also made it long."

There follow seven hundred and ninety poems, including

---

[21] A complete translation will be found in the Appendix.

specimens of every kind of epigram, and all, or almost all, having some smack of cleverness and wit. The author's animus against the Roman Church made him unsparing of ridicule and satire against priests, popes, and bishops. He uses also some of the stock subjects, such as misers, drunkards, and unblessed husbands. A number of the poems are merely versified jests like those written by More, as, for example, "Of a Certain Duke, and Robin Bartlett," "Of a Certain Bishop, and his fool Philibert," and "Of Robin Bartlett, fainyng himself deafe to get lodgyng, beyng on a time benighted."[22] In his satirical epigrams, Parkhurst frankly follows Martial. In fact, some of his imitations are so close that they suggest the exercises of a schoolboy to whom the task of paraphrasing or imitating has been assigned; and they may indeed be relics of Parkhurst's days at school. For example, Martial had written a monostich (viii, 19):

> Pauper videri Cinna vult; et est pauper.

> (Cinna wishes to appear poor, and he is poor.)

Parkhurst makes this easy adaptation under the title *In Fritonelum*:

> Vis morio videri: & es morio.

> (You wish to seem a fool, and you are a fool.)

Again, Martial had written (ix, 5):

> Nubere vis Prisco: non miror, Paula; sapisti.
> ducere te non vult Priscus: et ille sapit.

> (You wish to marry Priscus; I don't wonder, Paula; you are wise. Priscus does not wish to marry you: he, too, is wise.)

---

[22] These English titles are taken from Kendall's translations of Parkhurst, in *Flowers of Epigrammes* (1577).

Parkhurst's variant is headed *De Bunno & Polla*:

> Vxorem non vis Pollam, nec Polla maritum
> Te vult: Bunne sapis: nec minus illa sapit.

(You, Bunnus, do not wish Polla as a wife, and she doesn't wish you for a husband; you are wise, Bunnus—but she is no less wise.)

One further example introduces us to an epigram of Martial's (viii, 35) which became a favorite for imitation by English writers:

> Cum sitis similes paresque vita,
> uxor pessima, pessimus maritus,
> miror non bene convenire vobis.[23]

(Seeing that you are like one another, and a pair in your habits, vilest of wives, vilest of husbands, I wonder you don't agree!)

Parkhurst changed the metre without changing the point:

> Sat bene conveniet tibi cum Mopso Afra marito,
> Pessima es ipsa uxor; pessimus ille vir est.

In one epigram, not written in his school days, Parkhurst incorporates one of Martial's *verbatim*; I give Kendall's translation, without Parkhurst's Latin:

TO HERMANNUS MENNUS

> Poore haue I been, and poore I am,
>   and poore still shall I bee:
> And *Mennus* loe, the cause I will,
>   declare and shewe to thee.
> Martial. *If poore thou be Æmilian,*
>   *thou shalt be poore alwaies:*

---

[23] Parkhurst also made a longer epigram, expanding this one of Martial's; this, with other imitations, is discussed below.

For none but wealthy worldlyngs are,
enriched now adaies.[24]

It is clear that Parkhurst used Martial very much as More used the Greek Anthology; and while More shows almost no direct influence from Martial, Parkhurst shows as little influence from the Anthology.[25] He does furnish echoes of other Latin and Neo-Latin epigrams, particularly of those versified libels on popes and cardinals which were collected every year or so throughout the early decades of the century under titles like *Carmina quae ad pasquillum fuerunt posita,*[26] and which gave rise to the general terms *pasquil* and *pasquinade.*

For specimens of Parkhurst's work which cannot be so definitely referred to sources, let us notice his epitaph upon Sir Thomas Wyatt, dated 1542, in the last line of which he has employed the epigrammatist's favorite figure of paronomasia:

Musarum venerandus ille mystes
Hoc sub marmore conditur Viatus.
Cuius flent obitum Minerua, Phoebus,
Flent castae veneres, Amor pudicus,
Flent Pylo, Charites, novem sorores:
Et tu fleto Viator hunc Viatum.

~~~~~~~~~~

[24] *Flowers of Epigrammes* (Spenser Society reprint), p. 224. The italicized lines represent Martial's v, 81.

[25] Whipple, *Martial and the English Epigram*, p. 321n, lists six imitations of Martial from among Parkhurst's epigrams translated by Kendall; without having made this a matter of exact study, I should say that fifty or sixty more imitations or echoes could be recognized in the epigrams Kendall does not translate.

[26] In Parkhurst's *Ludicra* see, for example, *De Innocentio octauo Pontifice Romano*, and *De Alexandro sexto Pontifice Romano, & de eius filia Lucretia*, p. 83; these are referred respectively to distichs by Marullus and Pontanus, who were contributors to the *Pasquillus* collections.

Parkhurst also wrote an imitation of the Petronian epigram about the girl throwing a snow-ball, for which see above, p. 23.

(Under this stone is buried Wyatt, priest of the Muses, worthy of reverence; Minerva and Phoebus mourn his passing, modest graces and chaste love mourn, Pylo,[27] the Charites, and the nine sisters mourn: and do thou also, wayfarer, mourn this Wyatt.)

The epitaph upon Edward VI, the boy-king, is less conventional and embodies a felicitous conceit:

Cvm mors Eduardum rapuisset liuida Regem,
 Iunxisset superis cum Deus hunc*que* choris:
Iosias adit, amplexatur, eum*que* salutans
 Sic ait, o salue frater & alter ego.

(When pale death carried away King Edward, and God added him to the choirs above, then King Josias came and embraced him, with salutations, saying, "O welcome, brother, the other half of my soul!")

Others of Parkhurst's poems honor, either in life or in death, Queen Jane (Seymour), Queen Catharine (Howard), John Bale, John Leland, and several personal friends of no lasting renown. Upon the persecuting bishop, Bonner, he wrote these lines, which read as a compliment:

Omnes Episcopum esse te dicunt malum:
EGO tamen Bonere te dico bonum.

(Everybody says you are a bad bishop; but *I* say, Bonner, that you are a good one.)

The author's point comes out, however, in the title, *NEMO loquitur ad Edmundum Bonerum*—"*Nobody* addresses Ed-

---

[27] Pylo seems to be Nestor, used as a type of age and wisdom; but the form should be Pylus or Pylos. The Charities are the three Graces, whereas the *veneres* of the preceding line are "graces" or "beauties" used generally.

mund Bonner." Timothe Kendall, besides translating this gird, imitated it thus:

OF BONER

Of Bishops al, the *best* some did thee call:
Indeed thou wast the *beast* of bishops all.[28]

We may notice two other poems as illustrating further the variety of Parkhurst's writing. The first is merely a domestic jest addressed to his wife:

AD VXOREM, QUAE OLLAM PLENAM HERBIS IN
FENESTRA POSUIT

Vt sit odor fragrans, herbae plantatur in olla
Abs te: olidum ut crescant ingeris atque fimum.
Tolle fimum, vel tolle herbas, vt tollito vtrum*que*:
Quam bene olent herbae, tam fimus ipse male.

Kendall printed this translation in his *Flowers of Epigrammes* (1577):

To make a fragrant sauour sweet,
    in windowe thou dost set
Freshe flowers, and for to make them grow,
    thou stinking mier dost get:
Wife, cast the mier away, or herbs,
    or both I thee desire:
The flowers they doe not smell so well,
    as ill doth stinke the mire.[29]

---

[28] *Flowers of Epigrammes* (reprint), p. 292. The translation is at p. 228.
[29] Edward May, in his *Epigrams Divine and Morall* (1633) rewrote this translation in the more concise style of his time:

Faire flowers thou dost in thy window set,
And stinking dirt to make them grow, dost get.
Good wife cast all away, I thee desire,
The flowers smell sweet, but worser stinks the mire.

In changing "fourteeners" to pentameters May has sacrificed something of the sense, at least in the third line. That May did not use Parkhurst's Latin I attempt to show below, p. 102.

The second poem I have chosen is rather in the spirit of Horace, and will immediately suggest Robert Herrick's verses beginning, "Gather ye rosebuds while ye may":

IN QUASDAM EXIMIA FORMA PUELLAS, NIUE LUSITANTES

Cum niue ludatis, pura niue candidiores,
  Discatis quid nix candida significet.
Nix perit in vestris manibus, penitus*que* liquescit:
  Tempore sic paruo splendida forma perit.

Kendall translates thus:

OF CERTAINE FAIRE MAYDENS PLAIYNG WITH SNOWE

You virgins fairer than the Snowe
  wherwith you sport and play:
The Snowe is white, and you are bright,
  now marke what I shall say.
The Snowe betweene your fingers fades
  and melteth quight away:
So glisteryng gleames of bewties blaze
  in time shall sone decay.

Edward May, in his *Epigrams Divine and Morall* of 1633, made a free adaptation of this poem, and by introducing the mention of roses brought it one step nearer to Herrick:

TO CERTAINE MAIDENS PLAYING WITH SNOW

You tender Virgins, fairer then the Snow
            with which you play,
Note how it melts, thinke how the Roses grow,
            and how decay,
Just so does beauty fade, and age draw on,
Winter makes hast, and summer's quickly gone.[30]

[30] Herrick's poem is usually supposed, and probably with reason, to

Though Parkhurst's poems enjoyed some vogue, they evidently did not gain the wide reading or the influence which they would appear to have deserved. Four years after their publication, Timothe Kendall printed translations of eighty-seven of them, more than he translated from any other single author except Martial. Furthermore, Kendall suggests in these verses prefatory to his own *Trifles* (printed with *Flowers of Epigrammes*) that for the moment, at least, Parkhurst was the ranking English epigrammatist:

> *Borbon* in France beares bell awaie,
>   for writyng trifles there:
> In Englande *Parkhurst* praysed is,
>   for writyng trifles here.

After Kendall, however, Parkhurst's work almost disappears from view. John Weever printed in 1599 some epigrams based upon Kendall's translations from Parkhurst,[31] but he may not have known the *Ludicra* at first hand. Exactly the same may be said of Edward May, who in his *Epigrams Divine and Morall* (1633) included no fewer than fourteen pieces based upon Parkhurst;[32] but since all represent epigrams previously translated by Kendall, and since May uses many of Kendall's phrases, we may assume that he did not see the Bishop's book of Latin epigrams. After May, I find little trace of Parkhurst until the appearance of Robert Vilvain's *Enchiridium Epigrammatum* (1654), in which one of the longer epigrams from *Ludicra* is reprinted and translated. Thomas Fuller, of course, knew

---

have been suggested by the closing distich of Ausonius's idyl, *Rosae*:

> Collige virgo rosas, dum flos novus, & nova pubes,
>   Et memor esto aevum sic properare tuum.

There is every reason to suppose, however, that Herrick also had seen at least one of the three epigrams here reprinted.

[31] Weever's borrowings are noted below, p. 130.

[32] In May's First Century, Nos. 49, 50; in the Second Century, Nos. 14, 53, 56, 60, 67, 69, 70, 72, 73, 75, 98, 100.

Parkhurst, but only, or largely, through the account of him in Lawrence Humphrey's biography of Parkhurst's pupil and friend, John Jewel. Anthony à Wood evidently did read the *Ludicra*; for in addition to giving us the current uninformed opinion of the book, he states his own sound estimate:

"Which book, tho' written in his younger days, and contains therein more obscenity than the epigrams of Martial (as some say, tho' I myself cannot perceive it) yet while he was bishop he must needs have it printed, alledging that he would not be like Heliodorus to lose his bishoprick for it."[33]

Before leaving Parkhurst, for the sake of the record let us note that in spite of the word *Juvenilia* on the title-page of his book, and in spite of his statements that the epigrams were the work of his youth, a fair share of them were written when he was a mature man. A number of them bear dates, the earliest of which is 1537, when Queen Jane died in childbirth with Prince Edward. Parkhurst was twenty-five years old in 1537. At the death of Edward, which he also memorialized, he was past forty. When he speaks of his poems as the productions of his adolescence, he is thinking largely of his imitations of Martial and perhaps of the satirical ones generally—the ones to which exception might be taken. Also let it be said that Parkhurst translated more than half of the *Apocrypha* for the "Bishops' Bible" of 1568; and hence, although he published no sermons or other works in divinity, he was by no means neglectful of studies befitting a bishop. Why his epigrams did not become better known remains a mystery; they had good claims upon the attention of readers and, more widely circulated or more frequently translated, they might have hastened the process of acclimatizing in England the Martialian spirit.[34]

[33] *Athenae Oxonienses*, I, 413.

[34] Parkhurst's verses upon the beheading of Lady Jane Gray were copied into Egerton Ms. 2642, fol. 213v; there are commendatory verses by him

⟨ III ⟩

IN the next authors to be considered, Walter Haddon and George Buchanan, we have the two greatest British writers of Latin prose and verse, epigrams apart, in their century. Fuller relates that when Queen Elizabeth was asked which of these two she preferred, for learning, she "wittily and warily" replied, *Buchananum omnibus antepono, Haddonum nemini postpono*.[35] Haddon need not detain us long, however, for he wrote few epigrams. Most of his work in this kind consists of epitaphs, of which a number were included among his published *Poemata* (1567, 1576). For his anthology which appeared five years after the death of Haddon, Timothe Kendall made thirteen translations "Out of the Poemes of M. Gualter Haddon," but there is no satirical epigram among them, and three are extended catalogues of moral precepts. The following lines, "Of his owne picture," retain a modicum of point, even in Kendall's awkward English:

> (Foole as thou art) what dost thou mean,
>   thy fadyng forme to drawe?
> A newe face, or els no face, thou
>   shalt haue to morrow, daw.[36]

In the next century, Robert Vilvain, author of *Enchiridium Epigrammatum* (1654), found the distich of Haddon's worth quoting and translating, though he had lost track of its authorship.[37] He introduces it as "The 2 Verses which a

---

before Thomas Cranmer's *Aunswer . . . to Stephen Gardiner* (1580) and before Thomas Becon's collected works of 1560.

[35] *Worthies*, I, 206. The Latin may be translated: "I put Buchanan above everybody; I put Haddon below no one."

[36] *Flowers of Epigrammes* (reprint), p. 201. Haddon's Latin (*Lucubrationes*, 1567, p. 114) goes thus:

> Quid facis o demens, cur ora fugacia pingis?
> Aut nouus, aut nullus cras mihi vultus est.

[37] At fol. 167v. In Harl. Ms. 1221, a miscellaneous collection made

Divine made in death-bed, and caused to be inscribed on his Picture," and translates as follows:

Madman, what doost? why paintst thou flitting hew?
Thy face to morrow wil be none, or new.

The following lines, which, according to their heading, were translated from English into Latin, represent Haddon as an epigrammatist as well as any:

Sobria virgo, sibi quae vultu menteque constat,
    Et iuvenis frugi, veneris naufragia vitans,
Fidus, & aduertens coniunx, non pessima credens,
    Et mulier prudens, tractabilis atque pudica:
Quatuor haec quaerunt omnes, vix reperit ullus,
Maxima sic nostrae bona sunt rarissima vitae.[38]

An English version of these lines, attributed to Sylvanus Scorye, is preserved in Egerton Ms. 2642 (fol. 257r); from the manner of its entry there I should judge that this is not

~~~~~~~~~

largely in the time of James I, there is an anonymous translation, or adaptation, of Haddon's distich, with no reference to the original. It is at fol. 71r:

Workeman why takst thou care to carue in stone
That face which next day will bee new or none.

Haddon's Latin is copied out in Tanner Ms. 169 (fol. 147v) under the heading, "Against a representation by Pictures," and with a date indicating the year 1616. It is followed by an exercise in paraphrase, thus:

Idem aliter
Forma bonum fragile; Vna mutabilis hora?
    Luce nova nulla est; vel nova luce nova.

The first stanza of Cowley's poem, "My Picture," in *The Mistress* seems to owe something to Haddon's epigram:

Here, take my *Likeness* with you, whilst 'tis so;
    For when from hence you go,
    The next Suns rising will behold
    Me pale, and lean, and old.
The Man who did this *Picture* draw,
    Will swear next day my face he never saw.

[38] *Lucubrationes*, p. 77.

[105]

the original which Haddon says he followed, but is rather an exercise in translation by Scorye:

> A Mayde of modest mynde
>   and sobre every waye
> And thrifty youthe that shones the wrackes
>   of vaulting venus playe
> A wise and feithfull ffeere
>   not forcyng every Lye
> A prudent and a gentle wieff
>   that will not wade a wrye
> Theis fower doo all men seeke
>   But seldome can they fynde
> So rare is euery perfect gifte
>   In this oure wretched kynde.

Fuller records a "poetical pass" between Haddon, when a student, and Dr. Cox, his schoolmaster. It appears that at a time when Haddon was ill and unable to perform his scholastic duties, he addressed these lines to his teacher:

> Vix caput attolens e lecto scribere carmen
>   Qui velit, is voluit, scribere plura, Vale.

> (He who, hardly lifting his head from his pillow, wishes to write a poem, has wished to write more, —farewell.)

Cox's reply was:

> Te magis optarem salvum sine carmine, fili,
>   Quam sine te salvo, carmina multa, Vale.

> (I should much prefer to see you well and songless, my son, than healthless and with many songs, —farewell.)

The incident inspired Fuller, a century later, to add a distich of his own, which he gives in Latin and in English:

Praeceptor doctus, docilis magis an puer ille?
Ille puer docilis, praeceptor tu quoque doctus.

Master more able, child of more docility?
Docile the child, master of great ability.[39]

Haddon seems to have been much in demand for writing
epitaphs, commendations, inscriptions for pictures, and devices. He contributed to several of the volumes published
upon the deaths of famous persons, notably to the *Vita et
Obitus Fratrum Suffolciensium* of 1551. John Weever found
inscriptions of Haddon's making in St. Anne's Church at
Aldersgate.[40] As early as 1545, his commendation was
printed before the *Toxophilus* of Ascham. And his inscription for the banqueting house of Cobham Hall, as recorded
by Francis Thynne, found its way into Holinshed's *Chron-
icle* (1587).[41] The device which Haddon wrote for William
Hughes, Bishop of St. Asaph, also appears in Holinshed.[42]
After describing the bishop's arms, to which three stars had
been added by Queen Elizabeth, the chronicler says:

"Of which armes, namelie the three keies, and the three
starres, doctor Haddon composed these verses:

---

[39] *Worthies*, I, 199. This incident is also in Sir John Harington's "Supplie
or Addicion to the catalogue of Bishops" (1608), Park's *Nugae Antiquae*,
II, 107. The two distichs are among the *poemata* in Haddon's *Lucubrationes*, p. 80.

Harington says of Cox: "For our opinion of him in Cambridge, we held
him a good scholler, and a better poet than Doctor Haddon, who called
him Master."

[40] *Antient Funeral Monuments* (1631), p. 391.

[41] III, 1510. Haddon's Latin and Thynne's English rendering are quoted
by W. B. Rye, *England as Seen by Foreigners* (1865), p. 257. Both are
preserved in Addington Manuscript 37,666, fol. 39.

[42] Edition of 1808, IV, 770. It may be noticed that this device is considerably longer than the usual *impresa*, and is virtually equivalent to an
emblem, moralizing the coat of arms as an emblem moralizes a picture;
thus it illustrates the account of emblems as quoted from *The Arte of
English Poesie*, above p. 33.

Sunt antiquorum calues monumenta tuorum,
  Venit ab augusto principe stella triples:
Sic bene conspirant, virtus, doctrina, potestas,
  Et placidae pacis semina laeta ferunt.
Sed tandem ad finem decurrunt gaudia vitae,
  Ac homo puluis erit, puluis vt ante fuit."[43]

In all this, Haddon sustains his part as a scholarly rhetorician capable of turning out, upon whatever occasion, correct and sometimes eloquent verses. He was not, however, one of those who transmitted to England the authentic tradition of the epigram; and there is in him nothing of the austere grace of the Greeks or the savor of the Romans.

The epigrams of George Buchanan, "the learned Scot," have always been overshadowed by his more pretentious works, such as his paraphrases of the *Psalms*, his Latin dramas, and his history of Scotland. Yet some of his witty trifles, as we shall see, succeeding generations have treasured both in the original and in translation. Viewing his epigrams as a whole, we may observe that they were the by-products of some forty years spent in close relations with the scholastic, political, and religious life of France, Scotland, and England. The earliest collection of them to be printed bears the date 1566,[44] its author then being just sixty years old. About thirty epigrams, including some not in the first collection, were printed in 1569 with the second edition of the *poemata* of Théodore de Bèze (Beza). Finally, Buchanan's

---

[43] "The keys are the memorial of your ancestors, the triple star has come from our august prince: thus are happily met virtue, learning, and power, and these bear the joyful seeds of tranquilizing peace.

"But the joys of life come to an end at last, and man will be dust, as dust he was before."

[44] In *Franciscanus. Varia eiusdem authoris poemata*, n. p. The same group of epigrams, with some omissions and additions, was issued in 1568 under the title *Fratres Fraterrimi*, and was so reprinted in all later editions of Buchanan's poems.

epigrammata were classified and gathered into four books (the *Fratres Fraterrimi* and three others) and issued at Heidelberg in 1584, two years after the author's death, and reissued in 1594. During the seventeenth century there were several editions of all of Buchanan's Latin poems.

The three books entitled *Epigrammata* contain one hundred and eighty-three poems, the *Fratres Fraterrimi* twenty-seven, and there are about twenty-five epigrams among Buchanan's miscellaneous poems. Fourteen in the first book of epigrams and four among the miscellanies are translations from the Greek Anthology. The second book of epigrams is made up of a series of funeral verses, which Buchanan calls *justa* (obsequies), but which ordinarily would have been termed *epicedia* or *naeniae*; and a series of *icones*, verses for pictures or statues of gods and great men—and women, for there are here inscriptions for pictures of Queens Margaret of Navarre, Elizabeth of England, Mary of England, and Mary of Scotland. The epigrams of Buchanan's third book he classifies by using three other terms which we have not noted before: *strenae, pompae,* and *valentiniana.* The first are New Year's gifts (French, *étrennes*), and Buchanan's poems so named undoubtedly were sent as greetings to the persons named in their titles. His *pompae* appear to be verses written for processions: one set here was composed for a procession of gods and knights at the marriage of Mary, Queen of Scots; a second set was for "a procession of rustic gods bringing gifts to James VI and to Mary, his mother, at a dinner which followed the baptism of the King." Each epigram represents the speech of a member of the procession. The term *valentiniana* is of obvious meaning.

Among the scholars and literary men whom Buchanan honors are Roger Ascham, Bishop John Jewel, Julius Caesar Scaliger, Guillaume Budé, Johan Sturm, and Charles Utenhove. He addresses an epigram also to John Major (or Mair), a famous Scottish schoolman who had been his teacher at the University of St. Andrew's; but it is not encomiastic, for Buchanan had outgrown the scholastic and religious conservatism of Major. This epigram plays on a phrase which Major had applied to himself, *Joannes solo cognomine Major* (Major in name only):

> Cum scateat nugis solo cognomine Major,
>> Nec sit in immenso pagina sana libro:
> Non mirum titulis quod se veracibus ornat:
>> Nec semper mendax fingere Creta sola.

> ("Major by name," thou sayst, "and not by nature!"
>> The greatest liars sometimes speak the truth:
> And in thy endless stream of idle chatter,
>> What wonder if thou once hast spoken sooth!)[45]

Upon the death of Florence (?) Wilson (Florentius Volusenus), another Scottish Humanist, Buchanan wrote this excellent sepulchral epigram:

FLORENTIO VOLUSENO SCOTO

> Hic Musis Volusene jaces carissime, ripam
>> Ad Rhodani, terra quam procul a patria?
> Hoc meruit virtus tua, tellus quae foret altrix
>> Virtutum, ut cineres conderet illa tuos.

> (Here by Rhone's banks (from thy own fields how
>> far!),
>> Beloved of all the Muses, dost thou sleep:
> Yet doth the land that did thy virtues rear,
>> Meetly, O Florence, thy dear ashes keep.)

Buchanan stands virtually alone among the epigramma-

---

[45] The subjoined translation, and others from Buchanan quoted below without reference, are by P. Hume Brown, *George Buchanan* (Edinburgh, 1890).

With respect to the manner of satire adopted in this epigram, compare du Bellay's on Nicholas Bourbon, quoted below, p. 125.

tists considered in this chapter in having written true amatory epigrams, after the manner of the Greeks or of Catullus. The pages of Book I of his *Epigrammata* and those of his *Miscellanea* are strewn with verses *In Leonoram* and *Ad Neaeram*. In Book II of the *Epigrammata* is found his charming and fanciful *Amor*, which has been compared with Shakespeare's song in *The Merchant of Venice*, "Tell me where is Fancy bred."[46] A much closer parallel, however, is the Earl of Oxford's poem, "Of the birth and bringing up of Desire," which may safely be called a free adaptation of Buchanan's poem. Beside other details, Oxford takes over the main point, as a comparison will show. I give Buchanan's Latin, a close modern translation, and Oxford's poem as first printed in *Breton's Bower of Delights*, 1591:

AMOR

Quis puer ales? Amor. Genitor quis? Blandus ocelli
    Ardor. Quo natus tempore? Vere novo.
Quis locus excepit? Generosi pectoris aula.
    Quae nutrix? primo flore juventa decens.
Quo nutrit victu? Illecebris, vultuque venusto.
    Qui comites? Levitas, otia, luxus, opes.
Cur puero belli semper furiosa cupido?
    Impellunt avidae spes, trepidique metus.
Non metuit mortem? Non. Quare? Saepe renasci,
    Saepe mori decies hunc brevis hora videt.

LOVE

What winged boy art thou? Love is my name.
Who is thy sire? A glance's kindly flame.
When wast thou born? With the first vernal blossom.

---

[46] *Notes and Queries*, 4th ser., XII (1873), 406. For another close parallel, besides the one given in the text, see Sonnet XLIII of Griffin's *Fidessa* (1596), beginning, "Tell me of love, Sweet Love, who is thy sire?"

Thy home? The hall of a great-hearted bosom.
Who nursed thee? Comely youth in early grace.
And with what fare? With charms of winning face.
Thy comrades? Splendour, ease, wealth, joyance,
    light.
Why hath a boy such fierce desire to fight?
My greedy hopes impel and trembling fears.
Hast thou no dread when dismal death appears?
None. Why? Because before this brief hour fly
As oft as ten times do I live and die.

OF THE BIRTH AND BRINGING UP OF DESIRE

When wert thou born, Desire? In pomp and prime
    of May.
By whom, sweet boy, wert thou begot? By Good
    Conceit, men say.
Tell me, who was thy nurse? Fresh Youth, in
    sugared joy.
What was thy meat and daily food? Sad sighs,
    with great annoy.
What had you then to drink? Unfeigned lovers'
    tears.
What cradle were you rocked in? In hope devoid
    of fears.
What brought you then asleep? Sweet Speech,
    which likes men best.
And where is now your dwelling-place? In gentle
    hearts I rest.
Doth company displease? It doth, in many one.
Where would Desire then choose to be? He likes
    to muse alone.
What feedeth most your sight? To gaze on favor
    still.
Who find you most to be your foe? Disdain of my
    good will.

Will ever age or death bring you unto decay?
No, no! Desire both lives and dies a thousand times
    a day.[47]

As a more typical specimen of Buchanan's amatory epigrams
let me cite *De Neaera*, with three English versions, one
from each of the last three centuries:

> Illa mihi semper praesenti dura Neaera,
>   Me, quoties absum, semper abesse dolet.
> Non desiderio nostri, non moeret amore,
>   Sed se non nostro posse dolore frui.

> When with her, Neaera is always disdaining,
> As often, when absent, she is always complaining:
> Not for love of myself, to give bliss by consenting;
> But in both she is mov'd by her love of tormenting.

> When I am by her side, Neaera's cold,
>   And strange! she weeps when I am gone:
> Think not for love of me these tears she sheds;
>   At missing mine she sheds her own.

> Whene'er I come from greeting you refrain:
> Whene'er I go, capricious, you complain.

---

[47] The modern translation is by A. Gordon Mitchell, in *George Buchanan, Glasgow Quatercentenary Studies* (Glasgow, 1907), p. 46. Oxford's
poem is given as modernized in Hebel and Hudson, *Poetry of the English
Renaissance*, p. 104.

Buchanan's epigram may owe something to the several emblems of
Alciat which have to do with Cupid or statues of him; these have, for the
most part, the dialogue-form, and several of them were published as early
as 1531. Marullus also had written a dialogue-epigram describing the god
of love; two lines of it, from which Buchanan seems to have taken his
sixth line, follow:

> Quis cæcum præit? ebrietas, sopor, otia, luxus.
> Qui comites? rixae, bella, odia, opprobrium.

(Who goes before the blind god? Drunkenness, sleep, ease,
wantonness. Who are his companions? Quarrels, strife, hatred,
dishonor.)

It is not that to miss my face you deign,
And, loving, long for my return again:
   It is that then you cannot feast upon my pain.[48]

A French scholar of the seventeenth century was so taken by this epigram that, after translating it into French, he rewrote it in the form of an Italian madrigal.[49] Some of Buchanan's love-poems are "more condoling" than this; some are in looser language. At sixty, the author wrote to a friend "that he did not know whether to be chagrined or ashamed at the trifling character of the greater part of his poems." In 1579, he wrote in a letter that "but for the importunities of friends, he would have consigned to eternal oblivion, elegies, sylvae, and epigrams alike." Addressing Walter Haddon in a Latin poem written when he was nearly sixty, he makes these interesting confessions:

"In vain you challenge an old man to the sallies of his youth. Even in the years when such trifling is more seemly, rarely did the Muse visit me, born as I was in mountainous Britain, in a rude age, among a rude people. Now when declining age has left me a few white hairs, when I have all but told the tale of threescore years, and all my spirits droop, Phœbus turns me a deaf ear, and the Muses hearken not to my call. It yields me no joy now to sing how the golden hair of Phyllis is dearer to me than the locks of Bacchus, or to indite stinging iambics on Neaera's heartless want of faith."

Two questions growing out of Buchanan's amatory poems have caused some discussion. The first is whether the Leonora and Neaera of his poems represent real or fanciful

---

[48] The first translation is from *The Honeysuckle* (1734), the second by P. Hume Brown in *George Buchanan* (1890), and the third by F. P. Barnard in *A Fardel of Epigrams* (1922).

[49] *Menagiana* (Amsterdam, 1712), IV, 126. The madrigal is entitled *Pieta crudele*, and ends:

      Udir la cruda i miei sospiri ardenti,
      E mirar vuole i duri miei tormenti.

persons; the second, whether the Neaera and the Amaryllis of Buchanan were in Milton's mind when he wrote the passage in *Lycidas* which contains those names. To the first question we may give the usual answer when a poet's use of biographical material is under scrutiny: yes—and no. As for the second, while Milton knew Buchanan's poetry well, and borrowed from it in his Latin verses,[50] he hardly needed to learn the names Amaryllis and Neaera from the Scottish poet.

As the most widely current of all Buchanan's epigrams we must notice the oft-translated lines, *In Zoilum*, themselves a translation from the seventh *Epistola* of the Sophist Libanius:

> Frustra ego te laudo, frustra me, Zoile, laedis:
> Nemo mihi credit, Zoile, nemo tibi.

> (With industry I spread your praise,
> With equal you my censure blaze;
> But, Zoilus, all in vain we do—
> The world nor credits me nor you.)[51]

A recent translator has thus rendered it:

> Though you I praise, you me abuse, 'tis vain:
> For we can neither any credence gain.

---

[50] See the references listed under Buchanan's name in the Index of Walter MacKellar, *The Latin Poems of John Milton* (New Haven, 1930). See also the article by J. T. T. Brown in *George Buchanan, Glasgow Quatercentenary Studies*, 1907, pp. 61-90. Brown argues for the Miltonic authorship of a seventeenth-century translation of Buchanan's *Baptistes*; he also says, concerning the lines in *Lycidas*, that they "are by general agreement regarded as a passing allusion to the favorite nymphs of Buchanan."

[51] *Lebanii Opera*, ed. R. Foerster (Leipzig, 1921), x, 3:

Σὺ μὲν ἡμᾶς εἶπας κακῶς, ἡμεις δε καλῶς. ἀλλ᾿ οὔτε σοί τις οὔτ᾿ ἐμοὶ πείσεται.

Translation by Josiah Relph, whose poems first appeared at Glasgow, 1747. The two-line version which follows is by F. P. Barnard in *A Fardel of Epigrams*.

As we have noticed (p. 18), a translation of this epigram formed a popular song in France during the eighteenth century. Another French version was made by Le Brun, as follows:

> Par-tout je dis du bien de toi
> Par-tout tu dis du mal de moi,
> Nous prenons tous les deux, Zoyle,
> Une peine fort inutile,
> Personne a nos discours ne veut ajouter foi.[52]

A familiar anecdote concerning Voltaire embodies the point of Buchanan's epigram, a little altered:

"Grimm records how Voltaire one day asked an English visitor at Ferney from whence he had come.

'From Mr. Haller's.'

'He is a great man,' cried Voltaire, 'a great poet, a great naturalist, a great philosopher—almost a universal genius in fact.'

'What you say, Sir, is the more admirable,' replied the Englishman, 'because Mr. Haller does not do you the same justice.'

'Ah!' said Voltaire, 'perhaps we are both mistaken.' "[53]

An epigram of somewhat pathetic interest, in view of events which occurred subsequent to its occasion, is that written by Buchanan to accompany the gift of a diamond cut in the shape of a heart, sent by Mary of Scotland to Queen Elizabeth. This poem was printed in the author's third book of epigrams, and quoted, with others by Buchanan, in Camden's *Remains* (1605):

> Quod te jampridem fruitur, videt ac amat absens,
> Haec pignus cordis gemma, et imago mei est.
> Non est candidior, non est haec purior illo,
> Quamvis dura magis, non mage firma tamen.

[52] *Les epigrammes d'Owen tr. en vers francois* (Bruxelles, 1719), p. 203.
[53] S. G. Tallentyre, *The Life of Voltaire*, p. 349.

(The pledge and image of a heart
Whose constant joy and pride thou art—
This gem is not more fair, more pure,
Nor, though more hard, will more endure.)

We should notice some others among Buchanan's epigrams
to patrons, wherein he wittily, but undisguisedly, asks for
gifts. These expensive trifles were addressed to Queen Mary,
to James Stuart, Earl of Moray, and to the Earl of Lennox.
I quote two, the first of them addressed to the Queen:

Invida ne veterem tollant oblivia morem,
   Haec tibi pro xenio carmina pauce damus.
Sunt mala; sed si vis, poterunt divina videri;
   Nam nunc quod magno venditur aere, bonum est.

(A good old custom should not cease;
   Receive these songs, then, as of old.
Poor stuff? But good or bad is now
   Just what things fetch in weight of gold.)

The second was addressed to her brother, the Earl of Moray:

Sera Jacobe quidem sunt, pravaque munera nostra,
   Hac in re vitium si quod inesse putas:
Ne sectare meam, sed contra corrige culpam,
   Et cito, sed larga munera redde manu.

(Niggard and laggard came my gift, you say,
   Then must I deem your duty clear indeed;
By good example this my fault amend:
   Let thy gift come with bounty and with speed.)

Turning now to translators of Buchanan, we find that
Kendall, in his *Flowers of Epigrammes* (1577), rendered
into English only three of his poems, all of them from
Fratres Fraterrimi, which could well have been the only
collection to which Kendall had access. The epigrams put
forth under that title represent Buchanan's flings at the

Roman church and especially at members of monastic orders; they are his contributions to the great body of pasquinades. "Against Pope Pius," in Kendall's version, will serve to illustrate:

> *Pope Pius* heauen for money solde:
> Death will not let hym staie,
> In yearth: then needes to hell belowe
> Pope *P.* must take his waie.

A better translator was Francis Davison, who included in the second edition (1608) of *A Poetical Rhapsody* the following couplet based upon one of Buchanan's girds at Leonora. The title is Davison's:

ON A PAINTED COURTESAN

Whosoever saith thou sellest all, doth jest:
Thou buyst thy beauty, that sells all the rest.

Through the medium of a translation in *The Philosophers Banquet* (1614, 1636) Buchanan's *In Rusticum*, a low jest about a wood-cutter and his wife, passed into general currency.[54] It turns up again in Cotgrave's *Wits Interpreter* (1655).

In *A Banquet of Jests*, much in vogue throughout the 1630's,[55] there is narrated an incident which, whether true or false, throws light upon Buchanan's reputation as a skilful epigrammatist:

---

[54] A word as to oral tradition: some twelve years ago the present writer was told this jest of Buchanan's by a woodsman engaged in chopping down a tree. Evidently the story has been in lively currency among followers of the occupation from which its subject is drawn.

[55] Copies are extant of the first edition, 1630; fourth edition, 1634; fifth edition, 1639; and sixth edition, 1640. Also, another collection with the same title, distinguished as "the second part," appeared in 1633 and was reprinted at least once. My quotation is from the first part, edition of 1639.

OF BUCHANAN

"The famous poet *Buchanan* in his travels, was taken hold of by some of the Popes Inquisitors, who by his free writing suspected his religion; but he to acquit himselfe, wrote unto his Holinesse this Dysticon:

Laus tua, non tua fraus, virtus, non copia rerum,
Scandere te fecit hoc decus eximium.

Which I thus paraphrase.

Thy praise, not fraud, thy vertue not thy store,
Made thee to climbe that height which wee adore.

"For which *Encomium* hee was set at liberty, and being gone out of the *Popes* jurisdiction, hee sent to his Holinesse, and descried according to his owne true meaning, to read the selfe same verses backward, which were these:

Eximium decus hoc fecit te scandere rerum
Copia, non virtus, fraus tua, non tua laus.

"Thus Englished:

The height which we adore what made thee climbe?
Not vertue nor thy worth, rather thy crime."[56]

The presence of this story in this and other collections of jests, together with other traces of Buchanan's humor which persisted, will help to account for the strange fate which befell, in the eighteenth century, the poet's reputation among his own countrymen. In the folk-mind he became identified as a humorist, as King James's fool as well as tutor and counsellor. He is so described in a chapbook which first appeared about 1770, *The Witty and Entertaining Exploits of George Buchanan*, supposed to have been compiled by

[56] Abraham Fraunce, *The Arcadian Rhetorike* (1588?) fol. E3ᵛ, gives the Latin distichs with the heading 'Philelphus of Pope Pius.'

Dougall Graham, a hunchbacked bellman and writer of books for the vulgar. Such accidents of fame, however, have been too numerous for this one to excite surprise, particularly in view of the fact that Buchanan was, after all, an epigrammatist.

The most extensive translator from Buchanan in our period was Thomas Heywood, who published English renderings of four epigrams in *Pleasant Dialogues and Dramma's* (1637), one of them being another poem, longer than that we have quoted, sent with Mary's gift of a diamond to Queen Elizabeth. It has generally been overlooked that two other translations from Buchanan are embedded in the fourth book of *The Hierarchie of the Blessed Angells* (1635) immediately after the well-known passage upon the nicknaming of modern poets (p. 206).

"Heare but the learned *Buchanan* complaine," Heywood begins (with what seems to us a strange accentuation of our author's name), and then translates, with some freedom, the closing twenty-five lines of Buchanan's first elegy, *Quam misera sit conditio docentium literas humaniores Lutetiae*. In the course of the translated passage will be found a couplet which, after improvement, became an independent epigram of wide currency in this form:

> Seven wealthy towns contend for Homer dead,
> Through which the living Homer begged his bread.

Heywood's couplet is this:

> Seuen Cities warr'd for *Homer* being dead;
> Who liuing, had no roofe to shrowd his head.

The corresponding distich in Buchanan's elegy ran thus:

> Bella gerunt urbes septem de patria Homeri:
> Nulla domus vivo, patria nulla fuit.

Interestingly enough, before Heywood wrote, Thomas Nashe had singled out these two lines of Latin and treated them as an independent epigram. A passage in *Nashes Lenten Stuffe* (1599) follows:

". . . and to this effect hath Buchanan an epigram:

Urbes certarunt septem de patria Homeri,
  Nullo, domus vivo patria nulla fuit.

Seven cities strove, whence Homer first should come,
  When living, he no country had nor home."

I have not been able to discover the first appearance of the couplet in its last and most familiar form, though there is evidence that Dr. Thomas Seward (1708-1790) is responsible for it.[57]

The other example of Heywood's borrowing will illustrate the translator's freedom and occasional smoothness of verse. Buchanan's Latin is itself a translation, from a few lines of Theognis:

Nemo meas cumulet violis fragrantibus umbras,
  Nec mihi Pyramidum mole sepulchra locet.
Si quis amat, vivo largum se praestet amico,
  Talibus oficiis dum locus esse potest.
Verum ubi consumtos Lachesis mihi finiet annos,
  Vel fracta incultis horreat urna rubis.

None with fresh Violets my Ashes grace,
Or strow sweet fragrant Roses in the place.
If any loues me, and intends to giue?
I wish to taste his bounty whilest I liue.
What care I, when the Fates my Thread haue spun,
Though Briers and Thornes my Grace shall ouer-
  run.

Two of Buchanan's epigrams were translated into German

[57] See *Notes and Queries*, 2nd ser., IX (1860), 206, 293; Dodd, *The Epigrammatists* (1876), p. 397.

by Opitz and included in his *Florilegium variorum epigrammatum*, published in 1638.[58] Le Brun placed eighteen French translations from the Scottish poet after those from Owen in *Les Pensees ingeniuses ou les Epigrammes d'Owen*, Paris, 1710. The scattered English translations which appeared late in the seventeenth century and throughout the eighteenth are too numerous to record. It can be said that no anthology of epigrams (and there were many printed during the period referred to) failed to include some translated or imitated from Buchanan. We should notice, however, the one complete translation of all his epigrammatic works, made by a fellow-countryman, Robert Monteith, and published at Edinburgh in 1708, with the title, *The Very Learned Scotsman, Mr. George Buchanan's Fratres Fraterrimi, Three Books of Epigrams, and Book of Miscellanies, In English Verse; With the Illustration of the Proper Names, and Mythologies therein mentioned*. Monteith's versions are for the most part pedestrian, and for all of Buchanan's best poems one can find more spirited and poetic translations.

It would be possible to fill several pages with tributes to our poet's excellence as a writer of Latin verse. Above all other British writers whom we have occasion to notice, Buchanan was able to carry over into his borrowed language some of the genuine poetic eloquence and spirit with which he was endowed. Let me quote Henry Peacham, whose tribute to Sir Thomas More we have already seen, as an early English admirer of Buchanan:

"Of Latine Poets of our times in the judgement of Beza and the best learned, Buchanan is esteemed the chief. . . . His Tragedies are loftie, the stile pure, his Epigrams not to be mended, save heere and there (according to his Genius) too broad and bitter."[59]

---

[58] Gilbert Waterhouse, *Literary Relations of England and Germany in the Seventeenth Century* (Cambridge, 1914), p. 60n.

[59] *The Compleat Gentleman* (1622, etc.), reprint (Oxford, 1906), p. 91.

≺ IV ≻

WE cannot omit notice of some foreign writers who were in especially close relationship with the learned public of England. Erasmus and Buchanan, both of them men of more than one nation, we have already discussed. A slighter figure was Nicolas Bourbon (1503-1550), called *l'Ancien* in distinction from Nicolas Bourbon *Le Jeune* (1574-1644), a French writer whose reputation rests entirely upon his Latin poetry in *Nugae* (1533, 1538), later enlarged to *Nugarum libri octo* (1540). For several years, evidently from 1532 to 1536,[60] Bourbon was living in England and acted as tutor to several young gentlemen, one of them being Henry Norris, son of the Sir Henry Norris who was executed in 1536 as the alleged lover of Queen Anne Boleyn. The French scholar addressed encomia to several prominent Englishmen, notably to Thomas Cranmer, Hugh Latimer, Thomas Cromwell, and the Duke of Richmond, King Henry's illegitimate son who died in 1536. But most notable among the poems which Bourbon wrote in England are the objurgatory epigrams in Latin and Greek expressing the author's satisfaction in the downfall and execution of Sir Thomas More. I wish to quote Marsden's summary of these poems:

"The reflections made by Borbonius upon More's character and memory are extremely bitter and utterly devoid of wit. He makes several awkward attempts to play upon the Greek word μωρός [fool]—which is assumed as the Graecized form of the name 'More.' More is also represented as a man of low birth—'earth-born'—capriciously raised by Fortune to a false position of wealth and dignity. In that position he is

---

[60] His encomiastic epigram addressed to Cranmer upon his being made Archbishop of Canterbury may be dated 1532; his similar address to Cromwell upon his being given ecclesiastical power probably was written in 1535. Because of Bourbon's evident connection with the party of Queen Anne Boleyn, we may assume that he left England in the year of her fall, 1536.

represented as having demeaned himself both towards the people and towards the King in the spirit of a tyrant and in a manner hateful in the sight of God. In his presumption he dared to say that he was beyond the reach of fate. But the neck of the wretched man has lately come under the stroke of the axe. The bubble was not long in bursting."[61]

It should be noticed that besides being able to curry favor with the Queen and her party by denouncing More, Bourbon may well have had some motives arising from More's controversy with Germain de Brie, a compatriot and fellow-poet whom Bourbon praised in at least two epigrams.[62]

That the French epigrammatist was read and admired in England is evidenced by Leland's two complimentary epigrams addressed to him, and by the references to Bourbon, as the leading epigrammatist of France, in poems by Bartholomew Traheron and Timothe Kendall in Kendall's *Flowers of Epigrammes* (1577). Kendall went further: not only did he call his own contributions to his volume "Trifles" in imitation of Bourbon's title *Nugae*, but he also borrowed freely from the earlier writer. More than twenty of his short poems appear to be direct translations from Bourbon, and in no case is the source mentioned. As has been said, "in Kendall's time—and not in England only—what a man had translated was his own."[63]

We should notice also that the title of Bourbon's volume

<hr>

[61] *Philomorus*, pp. 261-262.

[62] In view of what has just been said it may be interesting to note that among Bourbon's poems are three which imitate or paraphrase three of More's. One of them is headed, *De solicita potentum uitae, Tale fere est epigraͣma apud Thomam Morum.* In the other two instances, Bourbon makes no mention of his model; his *In Uxores* follows one of the same title by More, and his *Vita humana cursus ad mortem* follows More's *Vita ipsa cursus ad mortem est.*

[63] The conclusion of James Hutton's article, "Timothy Kendall's 'Trifles' and Nicolas Bourbon's 'Nugae,'" *Modern Language Notes*, XLIV (1929), 19-22, wherein the relation of Kendall to Bourbon was first treated.

gave rise to witticisms thus expressed in a Latin and a French epigram by Joachim du Bellay:

Paule, tuum inscribis *Nugarum* nomine librum:
In toto libro nil melius titulo.

Bourbon, dans ses oeuvres nouvelles,
Ne montre pas un grand talent;
Mais, en les nommant *Bagatelles*,
Il fait preuve de jugement.

Early in the next century, these jests were imitated in a Latin epigram by John Owen (i, 42), thus translated by Thomas Pecke (*Parnassi Puerperium*, 1659):

UPON THE POET BORBONIUS HIS TOYES

You call your verse Trifles: be they so?
Ask yourself priuately, and you'll hear, No.
I shall refrain my verdict; yet I may
Take leaue to think, what you thought good to say.

Another French writer of Latin epigrams who exercised some influence in England was Théodore de Bèze (1519-1605), usually known by his Latinized name of Beza. After a period of some licentiousness in his youth, particularly while studying law at Orleans, Beza became a leader of both Protestantism and scholarship in France, the heir to Calvin's powers at Geneva. His *Juvenilia*, published in 1548 under the disguised name of Deodatus Seba, represents his literary wild oats; some poems in it he never allowed to be reprinted during his lifetime. Although their author might not have considered this fact important, we must note that English translations of nine poems from *Juvenilia*, some of them epigrams and others elegies, appeared in the first edition (1557) of *Songes and Sonettes*, now generally known as "Tottel's Miscellany."[64] Since the translator was Nicholas

---

[64] See H. H. Hudson, "Grimald's Translations from Beza," *Modern*

Grimald, the greater part of whose contributions were omitted from all editions of *Songes and Sonettes* after the first, only four of Beza's poems are represented in the miscellany as it became widely known through its numerous reissues. Three of the four poems are epigrams; and one of them, translated as "Description of Vertue," well represents both the Neo-Latin writing of the period and the first somewhat awkward attempts to exemplify in English the virtues of the epigram. Beza's poem suggests the *Amor* of Buchanan (quoted above, p. 111) and the various classical or Alexandrian epigrams which were written as a dialogue between the spectator and the figure represented by a statue or picture:

DESCRIPTIO VIRTUTIS

Quaenam tam lacero uestita incedis amictu?
　Virtus antiquis nobilitata sophis.
Cur uestis tam uilis? Opes contemno caducas.
　Cur gemina est facies? Tempus utrunque noto.
Quid docet hoc frenum? Mentis cohibere furores.
　Rastros cur gestas? Res mihi grata labor.
Cur uolucris? Docea tandem super astra uolare.
　Cur tibi mors premitur? Nescio sola mori.

Grimald translated thus:

What one art thou, thus in torn weed yclad?
Vertue, in price whom ancient sages had.
Why, poorely rayd? For fadyng goodes past care.
Why doublefaced? I mark eche fortunes fare.
This bridle, what? Mindes rages to restrain.
Tools why beare you? I loue to take great pain.
Why, winges? I teach aboue the starres to flye.
Why tread you death? I onely cannot dye.

Language Notes, xxxix (1924), 388-394, or the notes to H. E. Rollins, *Tottel's Miscellany* (1928-29).

Again, Beza had written an epitaph for one of the French king's counsellors:[65]

> Extincto nuper Respublica moesta Valente
>   Visa mihi secum sic gemebunda queri:
> Saepe alios fleui, dum sic raperentur, alumnos:
>   Causa tamen nunquam iustior ulla fuit.

Grimald applied the epitaph to Henry Fitzalan, Lord Maltravers, a promising and scholarly youth who died in 1556 while on his way abroad as ambassador to the King of Bohemia:

> Mee thought, of late when lord Mautrauers dyed,
> Our common weal, thus, by her self shee cryed:
> Oft haue I wept for mine, so layd a sleep,
> Yet neuer had I iuster cause to weep.[66]

And, finally, Beza's brief tribute to Titus Livius,

> Tumulum Tito nuper parabam Liuio,
> Quum sic Apollo iussit ut desisterem,
> Haec mortuos, inquit, decent, uiuit Titus,

Grimald applied to Cicero:

> For, Tullie, late a toomb I gan prepare:
> When Cynthie, thus, bad mee my labour spare:
> Such maner things becoom the ded, quoth hee:
> But Tullie liues, and styll alyue shall bee.

Among the poems from Beza which appeared in the first edition only of *Songes and Sonettes*, there is one which calls for special attention because of its illustration of the strained

---

[65] His name, on the evidence of Beza's title, was Jean Valence, or Valente.

[66] The genuine sense of loss felt by learned men on this occasion is evidenced by Walter Haddon's Latin elegy upon Lord Maltravers's death (also translated by Grimald), taken with Roger Ascham's reference in *The Schoolmaster*.

conceits, especially with reference to grief, which often found a place in Neo-Latin epitaphs, epigrams, and threnodies; that such writing had a considerable influence upon English poetry of the same and related sorts, we can well believe. Beza, among several poems upon the death of Guillaume Budé, French scholar and Reformer, had written:

> Budaeum fleuere homines, plorauit & aer,
> Budaeus gelidis est quoque fletus aquis:
> Sic fleuere homines, ut plena uolumina moestis
> Carminibus quiuis Bibliopola terat.
> Sic aer luxit, consumptis undique nimbis,
> Vt iam quas plueret non reperiret aquas.
> Flumina sic flerunt, ut qua modo nauis abibat,
> Currat inoffensis sicca quadriga rotis.
> Restabant caelum & tellus, communis ut omni
> Quanlibet immenso moeror in orbe foret,
> Sed quum caelum animam Budaei, terra cadauer
> Possideat, quaeso, qua ratione fleant?

Grimald translated this as a tribute to Sir James Wilford, who died in 1550 after a brief but brilliant military career in Scotland:

> For Wilford wept first men, then ayr also,
> For Wilford felt the wayters wayfull wo.
> The men so wept: that bookes, abrode which bee,
> Of moornyng meeters full a man may see.
> So wayld the ayr: that clowds consumde, remaynd
> No dropes, but drouth the parched erth sustaynd.
> So greeted floods: that, where ther rode before
> A ship, a car may go safe on the shore.
> Left were no mo, but heauen, and erth, to make,
> Throughout the world, this greef his rigor take.
> But sins the heauen this Wilfords goste dothe keep,
> And earth, his corps: saye mee, why shold they weep?

After pointing out the conceits in some others of Beza's poems, a learned commentator writes: "But all these will appear as remarkably plain, once we have before our eyes this other epitaph, *Budaeum flevere homines, etc.* . . . It is hardly credible that anyone could have attained to such silliness and ineptitude."[67]

Yet the next translator of Beza, Timothe Kendall, chose this same epitaph as one of the fifteen selections by which the French scholar is represented in *Flowers of Epigrammes* (1577). Kendall made a new translation of it,[68] retaining Budé as the subject, although he reprinted Grimald's version of *Descriptio virtutis* and adapted the lines Grimald had applied to Cicero. In this last instance, again, Kendall restored the lines to their original subject:

OF TITUS LIUIUS

For *Liuie* late a Tombe I gan ordaine,
    what meanest thou *Apollo* said, refraine:
Such maner things become the dead (q_d he)
    but *Liuie* liues, and still aliue shalbe.

Among the lighter poems translated by Kendall is one which well represents Beza in his Martialian vein. I give the English only:

TO CL. MAROTUS

Apelles learned hand, so fine
    did paint fair *Venus* Queene:
That euery one supposed that he,
    had *Venus* vewd and seen.
But workes of thine *Marotus* lewd,
    of *Venus* sauour so:

---

[67] L. Maigron, *De Theodori Bezae Poematis* (Leyden, 1898), p. 79; here translated.

[68] He probably had never seen Grimald's, as he reprints from *Songes and Sonettes* no poem that appeared in the first edition only.

That euery one sure deemes, that thou
dost all of *Venus* know.

John Weever, writing twenty years after Kendall, polished
and shortened this version and put it into his *Epigrammes*
(1599) with no reference to his predecessor; it is doubtful
whether Weever knew Beza's Latin:

IN SPURIUM QUENDAM SCRIPTOREM

Apelles did so paint faire *Venus* Queene,
That most supposde he had faire *Venus* seene,
But thy bald rimes of *Venus* sauour so,
That I dare swear thou dost all *Venus* know.

Another interesting appearance of Beza in England was
by way of a broadside published in 1588 as a part of the celebration of the Armada's defeat. On a large sheet was printed
a congratulatory Latin epigram by the then aged French
scholar, *Ad Serenissimam Elizabetham Angliae Reginam*,
accompanied by translations into English, Dutch, Spanish,
Hebrew, Greek, Italian, and French. At the bottom appeared a short epigram in French, "A l'Autheur de l'Epigramme Th. de Beze aagé presque de 70 ans." This was not
the only instance of printing epigrams on broadsides for
sale in the street, but it affords an interesting specimen of
the occasional liaison effected between scholars and the
popular audience. Another of Beza's more scurrilous epigrams appeared in English, translated by Francis Davison,
in *A Poetical Rhapsody* (1602), though without mention of
the source.[69] Still another, a dialogue-description of Religion, was put into English by Thomas Heywood for his
Hierarchie of the Blessed Angells (1635, p. 322); and the
same translator made English versions of ten more of Beza's
epigrams for his *Pleasant Dialogues and Dramma's* (1637).

[69] *In Aulam*, Bullen's edition of the *Rhapsody* (1891), I, 99.

Without pursuing further the English translations,[70] we have said enough to indicate that the learned public of England enjoyed some acquaintance, throughout the period we treat of, with the Latin poetry of Beza.

≺ V ≻

AMONG the less important English writers of Latin epigrams in the sixteenth century, we should notice three in especial: Sir Thomas Chaloner, Thomas Drant, and Thomas Newton. Thomas Drant will be reserved for treatment in a later chapter, since his English epigrams seem to have attracted more attention than did his Latin ones. Chaloner was a soldier and diplomat whose literary labors failed to win for him the posthumous reputation he would appear to deserve. Besides giving to Englishmen, in their tongue, *The Praise of Folly* (1549) and a homily of Chrysostom's (1544), he composed, while in Spain from 1562 to 1564, a long Latin poem concerning the history of England. With this poem, *De Rep. Anglorum Instauranda libri decem*, published posthumously in 1579, there appeared *Miscellanea, cum epigrammatis ac epitaphis nonnullis,* comprising Chaloner's occasional and lighter poems. The author did not cultivate the epigram, and most of the pieces in his collection are too long for this classification. His spirited attack *In Astrologomastigas,* for example, runs to twenty-six lines. Chaloner wrote, however, a satirical epigram of the purest type in his *Ad Rufum medicum,* and his epitaph upon Sir John Cheke, in four lines, is compressed and pointed. He also composed an epitaph upon Thomas Phaer, the translator of Virgil.

---

70 John Ashmore included a couplet, translated from Beza's epigram upon Lucretia, in *Certain Selected Odes of Horace, Englished* (1621). In Tanner Ms. 306, fol. 145ʳ, are five of Beza's epigrams quoted in full, with English renderings; this translator preferred the erotic ones. In Add. Ms. 15,227, fol. 12ʳ, is a neat translation, by Thomas Evans, of Beza's epigram on Pope Paul IV, beginning, *Pane et aqua Paulus contentus.*

The published collection ends with an epitaph upon Chaloner himself, written by Walter Haddon.

Thomas Newton of Cheshire, a physician and country rector, when he gave to the public Leland's Latin poems (1589), joined with them a collection of his own under the title, *Illustrium Aliquot Anglorum Encomia*.[71] The names celebrated by Newton are for the most part those of forgotten personages. One of his longest poems, however, commemorates the return of Francis Drake from his three-years' voyage around the world; others honor Archbishop Whitgift, William Fleetwood, and William Fisher. A fair share of the fifty-three poems are commendatory epigrams which had already been printed before in books by the author's friends; there are, for example, the stanzas which he had written for John Higgins's expanded edition (1575) of Nicholas Udall's *Floures for Latine spekynge* and for Henry Lyte's translation of Dodoens' *Herball* (1578). The following verses addressed to William Hunnies, "most steadfast of friends," concerning John Stow, chronographer, will serve as a specimen of Newton's composition:

~~~~~~~~~~

[71] The writer upon Newton in *D. N. B.* failed to distinguish between works which Newton edited and those which he wrote or translated; hence he attributes Leland's collection to Newton. Also, he sets down the *Progymnasmata* (1589) of John Brunswerd (Brunsuerdus) as Newton's, though Newton again was responsible only for collecting these poems and seeing them through the press. This book of Brunswerd's would claim a place in the present chapter, were it not for the fact that the poems in it are nearly all too long to be accounted epigrams. One, in praise of Theophrastus, is held to eight lines. Another paraphrases and expands the well-known Greek epigram upon Opportunity. Brunswerd, who died in 1589, had been Newton's teacher in the school at Macclesfield. Warton (*History of English Poetry*, 1871, IV, 279n) says that Brunswerd's epitaph, "made by his scholar Newton, yet remains in the chancel of the church at Macclesfield:

Alpha poetarum, coryphaeus grammaticorum,
Flos παιδαγώγων, hac sepulitur humo."
(In this ground is interred the first of poets, the chief of grammarians, the flower of teachers.)

Anglica scire cupis solide quis Chronica scribat?
Stous id egregia praestat Hunisse fide.
Quottidie e tenebris is multa volumina furuis
Eruit, is mandat plurima scripta typis.
Ex nitida illius deprompsi ego Bibliotheca
Plurima, quae nobis nocte dieque patet.

(Do you wish to know who writes faithfully
the English chronicles? Stow is pre-eminent,
Hunnies, for his remarkable credibility. Daily
from the shadows of obscurity he rescues many
volumes; he commits to print numerous writings. I myself have gathered many things from
his exceptional library, which is open to us night
and day.)

Among other books mentioned are Christopher Ocland's
popular Latin epics, *Anglorum Proelia* (1580) and *Eliza-
betheis* (1589), and Newton's own edition (1577) of Stan-
bridge's *Vocabula*. Amidst the poems of Newton we find
one by William Camden, addressed to the Cheshire scholar
in praise of one of his translations. It is clear that Newton,
whom we know chiefly as the collector and editor of the
English translations of Seneca, *Tenne Tragedies* (1581),
was in his own time esteemed for his learning and scholarly
zeal. Thomas Warton admired his Latin verse, saying: "He
is, perhaps, the first Englishman that wrote Latin elegiacs
with a classical clearness and terseness after Leland."[72]

Roger Ascham wrote Latin poetry, mainly complimentary
verses to the King or Queen and epitaphs upon deceased
friends. The small collection of poems printed at the end of
Familiarum Epistolarum Libri Tres (1576) reveals that
shortly before his death Ascham was engaged upon a long
poem to Queen Elizabeth, intended for presentation on

[72] *History of English Poetry*, ed. Hazlitt (1871), IV, 279.

November 17, 1568, the tenth anniversary of her accession. None of his Latin poems is, properly speaking, an epigram; but his dialogue-epitaph upon Sir Anthony Denney, in Greek, is closely allied to the many dialogue-epigrams found in the Greek Anthology and elsewhere. Kendall translated one of Ascham's epitaphs, that on John Whitney, for his *Flowers of Epigrammes* (1577). Two other important schoolmasters of the time, Richard Willes and Christopher Johnson, we shall consider in the next chapter, since their work was peculiarly of and for the schools. Henry Smith (1550?-1591), the "silver-tongued" Puritan preacher, wrote a handful of Latin epigrams, which were translated, along with Smith's *Microcosmo-graphia*, by Joshua Sylvester; the translations were printed in 1614 with *The Parlement of Vertues Royal* and many times thereafter.

Names of other scholarly epigrammatists may be culled from the several collections of epitaphs and tributes honoring famous men who had died. One such collection, *Vita et Obitus Duorum Fratrum Suffolciensum* (1551), made in honor of the two sons of the Duke of Suffolk, has been mentioned in connection with Parkhurst. As there stated, this volume contained poems by eighteen scholars of Cambridge and sixteen of Oxford, among whom will be noted, except for the absence of Roger Ascham and John Jewel, virtually all the names which illustrated English learning in the middle generation of the sixteenth century.[73] A distich by one

---

[73] The Cambridge men were: *John Cheke, *Walter Haddon, Charles Willoughby, *Nicholas Carr, Edward Aglionby (Aglionbaeus), *William Buckley, John Hatcher, M.D., *Robert Wisdom, *Thomas Wilson, *Christopher Carlile, Oswald Metcalfe, Henry Wright, Edward Cooper, *William Day, *William Harrison, William Scott, *Thomas Browne, Edward Earthly, John Gwynn, William Temple, William Waterman, John Tyrell. (Asterisk indicates an article in *D. N. B.* Dr. John Hatcher was the father of *Thomas Hatcher.)

The Oxford men: *Nicholas Udall, Henry Knollys, Richard Barte (Bartaeus), *John Parkhurst, *William Overton, *Lawrence Humphrey,

of the poets of this volume, Armagil Wade, upon the death of Queen Jane Seymour, mother of Edward VI, reappears in a seventeenth-century collection of epitaphs, as follows:

Phoenix Iana iacet, nato Phoenice, dolendum
Saecula Phoenices nulla tulisse duos.

(Here lies Jane, a Phoenix, having given birth to a Phoenix: alas, that no age allows of two Phoenixes!)[74]

Poems occasioned by the death (in 1571) of Bishop John Jewel were issued with Lawrence Humphrey's Latin life of the bishop in 1573, with this half-title: *Odae, Epigrammata, Epitaphia, &c., in laudem & mortem Johannis Juelli, Episc. Sarisb.* To this collection Daniel Rogers, an epigrammatist we have not mentioned hitherto, contributed six sets of verses. Rogers was a diplomatist interested in advancing the cause of Protestantism; according to some accounts,[75] he had studied as a boy under the great Philip Melancthon, who was an epigrammatist as well as a reformer. A religious poem, in Latin, by Rogers was printed at Basle in 1567; the rest of his writings, except for some scattered epistles and the epigrams here noticed, remained in manuscript. Camden quoted one

---

*Michael Renniger, William Waterman, Theodore Newton, *John Molyns, John Biddle (Bidillus), George Kenn (Kennus), Henry Squire, James Calphil, Henry Gunvile (Gunvilus), John Day, Henry Grenville, *Armagil Wade, Thomas Pyre (Pirreus). (For Henry Knollys, see *D. N. B.*, art. Sir Francis Knollys.)

Among the miscellaneous poems included in the third section of the volume, I notice these additions: *William Cecil, *Anthony Cooke, *Thomas Chaloner.

[74] *Epitaphia Joco-Seria*, collected by Francis Swertius (Cologne, 1623), p. 157. The epitaph is not there assigned to any author and is incorrectly headed, *Ioannae Reg. Angliae.* The poem appears in Egerton Ms. 2642, fol. 213r, with the heading, "Verses made by Mr Armigill Wade, vppon the deathe of Qveene Jane, and vpon the Birth of Prynce Edwarde hir Sone."

[75] One is quoted in Bliss's edition of *Athenae Oxonienses*, I, 570-571.

epigram by Rogers in *Britannia* (1586), as a part of his description of the Cathedral of Salisbury:

> Mira canam; soles quot continet annus in una
>   Tam numerosa, ferunt, aede fenestra micat:
> Marmoreasque capit fusas tot ab arte columnas
>   Comprensas horas quot vagus annus habet.
> Totque patent portae quot mensibus annus abundat.
>   Res mira, at vera res celebrata fide.

> (Wondrous to tell, as many windows here,
> As solar revolutions in one year.
> As many marble pillars rise around
> As hours within the fleeting year are found.
> As many doors as months admittance give,
> Strange as it seems, we must the tale believe.) [76]

Rogers's epigram to the University of Oxford was printed with the description of Oxford made by Ralph Agas, the cartographer, in 1578.[77] It has been generally overlooked, however, that a voluminous collection of Latin poems by Rogers, including three books of epigrams, has been preserved to modern times in a manuscript in the library of the Marquis of Hertford.[78] Of the two hundred and forty-seven

[76] Text and translation from Richard Gough's version of the *Britannia* (2d ed., 1806), I, 133. In the second line of the English, 1806 misprints "revolution" for "revolutions."

Sir John Harington referred to Rogers's epigram in his "A Salisbury Tale," (IV, 36), which begins:
> Faire *Sarum's* Church, beside the stately tower
> Hath many things in number aptly sorted,
> Answering the yeere, the month, weeke, day & houre,
> But aboue all (as I haue heard reported,
> And to the view doth probably appeare)
> A piller for each houre in all the yeere.

[77] According to Wood, *Athenae Oxonienses* as before, I, 571; I have been unable to find the work referred to.

[78] A description, with titles and quotations, will be found in *Historical Manuscripts Commission, Fourth Report, Part I* (1874), Appendix, pp.

epigrams, the greater part are encomia or epitaphs upon contemporaries of the author—Buchanan, Haddon, Thomas Wilson, Queen Elizabeth, Melancthon, John Bale, and scores of others. One poem is "Good wishes for William Cecil, suffering from the gout." Another is addressed to Job Throckmorton, who, after Rogers's death, was to be imprisoned for his complicity in the Puritan "Mar-Prelate" conspiracy. Among Rogers's longer poems there are several written to and about Sir Philip Sidney during his lifetime; these might well be consulted by biographers of Sidney. Two epigrams, one of them in Greek, are addressed to Albrecht Dürer, the artist. Two celebrate the fame of Geoffrey Chaucer. I quote one of these:

Quantus erat Tusco Boccacius ore, favebat
Itala quantum olim lingua Petrarche tibi;
Qualis os insurgit Gallo sermone Marottus
Aptat dum patria verba poetae lyrae;
Tantus eras Galfride tuis Chaucere Britannis
Ingenio vates nec minus ore potens
Anglica quo veneris nunc spirat lingua magistro
Quas Italis, Gallis, ille vel ille dedit.

(As great as was Boccaccio in Tuscan speech, as much as of old the Italian tongue delighted in thee, O Petrarch, and as discourse in the French language grows elevated now that Marot fits native words to the poet's lyre,—thus much and so wert thou, Geoffrey Chaucer, among thy Britons; by genius a poet no less powerful over English speech; under this master our tongue now lives with those graces

252-254. Besides the epigrams, there is a book of elegies, a book of odes, one of *sylvae*, one of *hendecasyllaba*, and one of *urbes* or poems upon cities. This last is probably also a book of epigrams. At the end is a collection of poems addressed to Rogers by other poets.

which this man or that man gave to the Italians and
the French.) [79]

A few other obscure and forgotten epigrammatists remain
to be listed. According to Anthony à Wood, John White
(1510?-1560), bishop successively of Lincoln and of Winchester, wrote and published a book of epigrams, though it
has disappeared. Fuller says of him: "He was a tolerable
poet; and wrote an elegy on the eucharist, to prove the cor-
poral presence, and confute Peter Martyr, the first and last,
I believe, who brought controversial divinity into poetry."
White wrote congratulatory verses for the marriage of
Philip and Mary in 1554; these are quoted by Foxe, with
this comment: "Amongst all other, master White, then
bishop of Lincoln (his poetical vein being dronken with joy
of the marriage) spewed out certain verses."[80] These were
replied to by Parkhurst and others.

Again, we learn from Wood that John Clement, tutor of
Sir Thomas More's children, wrote *Epigrammatum &
aliorum carminum, lib. 1*; that John Hoker (M. A., Mag-
dalen College, 1535) wrote *Epigrammata varia*; that John
Fowler (1537-1579), a Catholic printer and scholar, wrote
"Epigrams and other verses," though these may have been
in English; and that Peter White (fl. 1562) wrote *Epigrammata diversa, lib. 1*. Richard Latewar (1560-1601), "a most
ingenious Latin poet," was a prominent contributor to
Exequiae (1587), a volume of Latin verse written by Oxford
men upon the death and fame of Sir Philip Sidney. Wood
(I, 710) reprints several of Latewar's epigrams. The death of
this scholar as a result of a wound received in Ireland,
whither he had gone as chaplain of Charles Blount, Lord

---

[79] The manuscript gives *suada* as an alternative, in the second line, for
lingua; it may be translated as "eloquence."

[80] *Acts and Monuments*, ed. Townsend (1846), VI, 555. White's yield-
ing to the change of religion under Mary accounts for Foxe's venom and
for Fuller's coolness a century later.

Mountjoy, gave rise to a punning epigram which passed into the tradition of Oxford humor:

> A sero bello dives durusque vocatus,
> A sero bello nomen et omen habet.

(Called *rich* and *hard* by *late war*, from the late war he received both his name and his doom.)

We have noticed one famous Scot, George Buchanan, and we shall have occasion to discuss other writers of his country. We should not omit to record that Irish scholars of the sixteenth century also cultivated the epigram. As will be seen, what happened was that the influence of studies in this kind spread to Ireland by way of the English Universities. The Peter White of the foregoing paragraph, for example, was an Irishman who, after receiving the degree of Master of Arts at Oxford in 1555, returned to his native land as a teacher.[81] Richard Stanyhurst, whose work we shall have occasion to mention, was one of White's pupils. Patrick Cusack (fl. 1566) also received his education at Oxford and then returned to be a schoolmaster in Dublin. He wrote, apparently for the use of his pupils, *Diversa epigrammata*, of which I quote a specimen; this was written evidently as a warning against cheating:

> Verba aliis si des, tandem tibi verba dabuntur;
> Fraus sequitur fraudem, corpus ut umbra suum.

(If you give words to others, words will be given to you; fraud follows fraud, as a shadow follows what casts it.)

James King died in 1569, while he was still a student at Cambridge; but he had written some Latin poems in praise

---

[81] These accounts of Irish writers are all taken from the thirteenth chapter of *The Writers of Ireland*, the second volume of *The Whole Works of Sir James Ware* (Dublin, 1745). This history, though mainly by Ware, was edited and continued by Walter Harris.

of Sir Henry Sidney, Lord Lieutenant of Ireland, and also *diversa epigrammata*. James Walsh (fl. 1575) was an M.A. of Oxford who also wrote "various epigrams." But as the historian we follow said: "Many other of these sort of writers I pass over."

⫷ APPENDIX ⫸

(Translation from John Parkhurst, *Ludicra siue Epigrammata Iuuenilia* (London, 1573); fols. A₁₁ recto to B₁ recto.)

TO THE READER

DEAR READER, long ago we wrote at odd times certain epigrams of many sorts, which, because we composed them by way of amusement and just to be doing something, we are pleased to call *ludicra*. Indeed we did not write them with the notion that they should ever be published and come into the hands of men (for why should they, especially the trivial and unpleasant ones, and those born, as it always seemed even to me, of angry Muses); but that by writing I might seduce from anxiety a mind sometimes weakened by sickness and cares, might refresh it in the meditation of trifles of this kind, and find it again more animated and more eager. Some years ago, while I was still in England, and in the earlier part of my stay in Germany, these epigrams had fallen into the hands of some of my friends; forthwith these friends, not so much influenced, I should judge, by the grace of the compositions themselves or the elegance of the verse (which for the most part is nothing), as warmed by their zealous affection for me, began importunately to urge that I give them to the world. I argued that the poems were light, immature, facetious, written for myself alone, not fitted to the times, unsuitable to my character, unworthy of the light, improper for the public. They prayed, solicited, urged, and multiplied entreaties, blandishments, importunities and contentions; and they said that the epigrams of Heywood and

Crowley, though written in their native tongue, were honored and held in great esteem. What would you have? At
length I was vanquished: I was drawn from my resolution;
I promised some time to publish. I say I promised, but in an
unwilling and reluctant spirit. For I do not love myself and
my works as Heliodorus, Bishop of Tricca,[1] is said to have
loved himself and his: for he (as Nicephorus relates) as a
youth had published some amatorious books, and this fact
the synod of elders deemed improper; when they gave him
the choice either to withdraw from his bishopric or to
destroy the books by fire, he preferred to throw overboard
his dignity rather than his books. Worthy, in truth, is such
a one to write good poems, since he holds them in such
price! If such a choice were given to me, indeed, I should
settle on much easier terms.

For beside the fact that I know there is not such talent in
my poems that they deserve to be esteemed, I do not doubt
that there will be those who will censure a great deal in this
little book. Some will complain that there are loose epigrams here, that there are trivial ones, that they are not to
be tolerated, that there was already enough of this kind of
poetry. To these, to be sure, I can truly reply either that there
are not so many of the objectionable epigrams that the whole
book should be damned on their account, or that they are
so restrained and corrected that anyone can see some consideration paid to modesty. However, the equitable critic
should remember that these were not written by a man who
was old and white-haired, not by a Stoic philosopher, but by
a young man, to whose age certainly something is usually
allowed; and I need not call to mind how the Martials,
Tibullyses, Catulluses, Propertiuses, as mature men did not

---

[1] A bishop of the first or second century who, by old accounts, was
author of *Aethiopica*, or, as generally referred to, "The Ethiopian Ro-
mance." Now this is thought to have been the work of another Heliodorus,
of Emesa, a sophist of the third century.

shrink from this kind of writing; how Plato himself, the greatest philosopher and soundest of men, at times laying aside philosophical severity and sternness, freely wrote a number of epigrams to his Stella. Of Thomas More, at one time Chancellor of England, a man pre-eminent in his times for his learning in Latin and Greek, I say nothing. For he wrote facetious poems in this kind, and loose ones, and indeed certain not particularly chaste ones, yet afterwards he was placed among the celestial heroes and now is reverenced with divine honors by those of his church.[2] To be sure, I do not covet an apotheosis such as his. But what in him could be tolerated and approved should not be condemned in others. For many poets of our own times have written in this kind, poets of renown and men of distinction. And if anyone thinks they should be condemned for their writings like mine, I can endure with no uncalm spirit being reprehended in their company. Some other critics, perchance, will not endure my satirizing with such liberty of speech the decrees of popes, their unadulterated frauds, and corrupted religion, and their profane and impious luxuries. To these I do not know anything to say but that a hard wedge is

---

[2] *tamen postea inter Diuos Indigetes relatus est, et nunc a suis diuino honore colitur*; an early reference to the beatification, then unauthorized, of More as one of the martyrs of the Church. The beatification was actually consummated by a Decree of Pope Leo XIII, "confirming the honor given to the Blessed Martyrs, John Cardinal Fisher, Thomas More, and others," issued December 29, 1886. (This decree is translated in full by Thomas Bridgett, *Life and Writings of Blessed Thomas More*, 1904.) Pope Leo there writes of More and Fisher: "Gregory XIII even granted in their honor several privileges appertaining to public and ecclesiastical worship; and chiefly that of using their relics in the consecration of altars, when relics of ancient Holy Martyrs could not be had." Gregory XIII was Pope from 1572 until 1585. If Parkhurst wrote this passage in 1558, it is evidence of the widespread honors paid More at a time long before the Pope gave recognition to them. On the other hand, Parkhurst may have interpolated this passage in 1573 after Gregory had granted the privileges spoken of.

needed for a hard knot,[3] and that I have always, from boyhood, hated those abuses. If to anyone I seem to assault too
bitterly the impure morals of certain priests, and their flagi-
tious pretence of chastity, let that one know that there have
been unworthy monsters of this sort who were painted in
better colors. Whatever I have done, I am not the first, nor
have I done it without a model. For not to speak of Paul's
naming men of that kind fools, dogs, gluttons, and foes of
the cross of Christ, our Lord Himself called them blind,
whited sepulchres, generation of vipers. Here and there
indeed I attack bishops, but lazy inactive ones, foes of the
gospel, *aposkopous, alaoskopous,* and anything whatever
rather than what they would like to pass for, *Episcopos.*
Other readers will complain that these poems are jesting
and inconsequential, while mourning and tears better suit
with our times. I know: and I confess and pray God
through Christ Jesus that He please in due season to vindi-
cate His name and send away this calamity from us. Yet
you should know that these poems were written in happier
days, and men, even pious men, used to mitigate the sadness
of their own days by some pleasantry of this sort. Another
says, perhaps, that such poems are of a low order and are
too facile. This I do not disguise, but I openly say that I

---

[3] Proverbial: cf. St. Jerome, *Epistola* lxix, 5: *interim iuxta vulgare pro-
verbium, Malo arboris nodo, malus cuneus requiriendus est*; also J. G.
Seybold, *Selectiora Adagia Latino-Germanica*, Nuremberg, 1683, p. 190,
Malo nodo malus quaerendus est cuneus. In Bartlett's *Familiar Quotations,*
10th edition (Boston, 1914), p. 898, "Look for a tough wedge for a
tough log," is given as Maxim 723 from Darius Lyman's translation of
Publilius Syrus. I have been able to find the Latin proverb in no collection
of the maxims of Publilius, though at various times a wide variety of
work has been attributed to this author.

This proverb seems never to have come into currency among English-
speaking people, as no collection of English proverbs records it. However,
the words of Ulysses in *Troilus and Cressida*, I, iii, 316, "Blunt wedges
rive hard knots," may have been derived from it.

have pursued such literary tasks by design. For I prefer that my writings, in whatever sort, be understood even by a reader of moderate learning rather than that they be neglected. Wherefore, friendly reader, take in good part these first fruits of my youth, and, if need be, refute the carpings of traducers.

Farewell. At Zurich, 1558.

CHAPTER IV · THE EPIGRAM IN
SCHOOLS AND COLLEGES

A READER of the preceding chapters cannot have escaped
the inference that Latin epigram-writing in England was
closely bound up with academic life. Although in the work
of More this connection was not strong, we recall that
William Lily was headmaster of St. Paul's School when he
engaged in epigrammatic controversy with Whittington,
while his ally, William Horman, was headmaster successively of Winchester and of Eton. John Constable acknowledges that most of his epigrams were written by him as a
student. Thomas Newton was for a time a schoolmaster.
And in the seventeenth century we observe that a headmaster of Warwick School, John Owen, described by Ben
Jonson as "a pure pedantic schoolmaster, sweeping his living
from the posteriors of his little children," came to be the
most widely read modern epigrammatist. English schools
have always required the composition of Latin epigrams as
an exercise in rhetoric; the purpose of this chapter is to emphasize this fact and to illustrate its effects, both inside and
outside the schoolroom.

◄ II ►

As far back as the twelfth century, we may learn from
William Fitzstephen's *Descriptio ... Londoniae,*[1] the writ-

---

[1] Fitzstephen (d. 1190?) prefixed the *Descriptio* to his biography of
Thomas Becket. John Stow printed the *Descriptio* at the end of *A Survay
of London* (1598). Stow's text is faulty; and I quote from *Materials for
the History of Thomas Becket* (Rerum Britannicarum Medii Aevi Scrip-

ing of epigrams constituted a school-exercise, or at least what
we should now call an extracurricular activity:

". . . Pueri diversarum scholarum versibus inter se con-
rixantur: aut de principijs artis grammaticae, vel regulis
praeteritorum vel supinorum, contendunt. Sunt alij qui epi-
grammatibus, rhythmis et metris, utuntur vetere illa triviali
dicacitate; licentia Fescennina socios suppressis nominibus
liberius lacerant; loedorias jaculantur et scommata; salibus
Socraticis sociorum, vel forte maiorum, vitia tangunt; vel
mordacius dente rodunt Theonino audacibus dithyrambis.
Auditores,

> multum ridere parati,
> Ingeminant tremulos naso crispante cachinnos."

(Boys of the different schools wrangle with each other by
means of verses; they dispute either about the principles of
grammar or about rules of preterites and supines. Some in
epigrams, rhymes, and meters practice old-fashioned street-
raillery: with Fescennine license they openly scourge their
fellows, though not mentioning names; they hurl abuse and
jeers; with Socratic witticisms they allude to the vices of
their mates or perchance of their elders; or in bold dithy-
rambs they slander with Theonine sharpness. Hearers,
though prepared to laugh much, 'redouble, with crinkling
noses, their peals of laughter.')

Passing to a later century, we find that young William
Paston sent home from Eton, in 1479, a specimen of his
epigrammatic versifying.[2] With the arrival of the New

tores, LXVII, III (1877), 5. J. C. Robertson, the editor, errs in making
multum ridere parati part of a quotation; only the five words following
this phrase are from Persius, III, 87.

'Fescennine' is an adjective derived from Fescennia, the name of an
Etrurian city famed for jeering dialogues in verse. 'Theonine' is an adjective from the name of Theon, a satirical poet.

[2] He wrote (*Paston Letters* [Bohn edition, 1849], p. 122):
. . . "And as for my coming from Eton, I lack nothing but versifying,

Learning, there was an attempt to extend the exercise to Greek composition. "And would you ever have believed it," wrote Erasmus in 1528, "that among the English and the Dutch, schoolboys babble Greek, and exercise themselves, not unhappily, in Greek epigrams?"[3] While Greek epigrams do turn up occasionally in the work of students and scholars, it is evident that versifying in Greek was not so generally required. As for Latin, an account of a typical day at Winchester College, about 1550, indicates that Martial was studied by three of the four forms and that "verse tasks" occupied practically all of the boys for two hours or more each day. Skipping a century, and passing to the University, we find that when Isaac Barrow took the office of Humanity Reader at Cambridge, in 1659, he referred to the writing of epigrams in his inaugural address. After giving advice to his prospective students concerning their themes, "the same," he said, "about your verses; and recollect that they are to be

---

which I trust to have with a little continuance.
>   Quare, Quomodo. Non valet hora, valet mora.
>   Unde di
>   Arbore jam videas exemplum. Non die possunt
>   Omnia suppleri sed tamen illa mora.
And these two verses aforesaid be of mine own making."
There has been some misinterpretation of this passage by editors who have tried to make a quatrain of the Latin, conjecturally filling out the second line, beginning with *Unde*. The *di* is inexplicable as it stands; by my reading I make it *dico*. Otherwise the passage is fairly clear. The boy had been assigned the task of applying the questions *quare* (why) and *quomodo* (how) to the "theme," *Non valet hora, valet mora*. Whence (*unde*) he produces the two verses which he claims. No editor has provided a translation for them, as the last four words are somewhat baffling. I suggest: "In the tree, now, you see an example. Not in a day can all things be supplied [can the tree come to full growth], but only through delay [through a slow process]." The learned Hallam wrote that "the specimen he (Master Wm. Paston) rather proudly exhibits, does not much differ from what we denominate nonsense verses." Probably young Paston's family could not read Latin.

[3] *Dialogus de Pronuntiatione*, in *Opera*, Leyden edition, I, 923, C.

epigrams, and must have some grace and point in them."[4] And to bring our record down to modern times, we may note that A. F. Leach records that when he was at Winchester, in the late nineteenth century, the boys had to produce three Latin epigrams a week.

The actual methods of using the epigram in school are revealed in several sixteenth-century documents. In general, the methods reduce themselves to two: first, the setting of a "theme," that is, a proverb or phrase, such as *Tempus edax rerum* (Time, the devourer of things), to be given restatement, application, or comment; second, the paraphrase or variation of a complete epigram from the Greek Anthology, from Martial, or from some other classical author.[5] We have a description of the first method in Erasmus's colloquy, "The Poetical Feast."[6] The author represents a group of friends informally competing in composition; but we may assume that the practice of the schoolroom was essentially the same. An umpire is appointed, and a subject is set. In this instance the subject is the statement, "He acts very preposterously, who has a Garden neatly trimm'd up, and furnished with various Delicacies, and at the same Time, has a Mind adorn'd with no Sciences and Virtues." Each competitor phrases the thought in Latin verse. Six versions, in varying meters, result. Then the proposal is made that the same contest be carried on in Greek, but only one Greek version is given before the exercise is interrupted and the umpire asked to give his decision. A practice virtually identical, carried on a century after Eras-

----

[4] *Theological Works of Isaac Barrow*, ed. Napier (Cambridge, 1859), IX, xvii. Translated and condensed by Napier; Barrow's Latin may be seen in the same volume, p. 134.

[5] We have seen illustrations of this method from the work of Parkhurst, above, pp. 96-98.

[6] *Colloquies of Erasmus*, translated by N. Bailey (1878), I, 318 ff. Note that here an epigram was not specifically required, and that the theme set is longer than those usually set for epigrams.

mus wrote, is described in an account of the exercises at Westminster School in the period 1621-1628: verses were required in both Latin and Greek upon two or three several themes, "and they that made the best two or three of them had some money given them by the school-master for the most part."[7]

A reader familiar with the literature of the sixteenth and seventeenth centuries will recall how this sort of exercise left its mark upon poetry. In the first place, we may notice that in many printed collections of epigrams, each poem is headed by a phrase or proverb—often in Latin, even though the epigrams are English—which is nothing but the "theme" as set in school. The several volumes by the most prolific English epigrammatist of the seventeenth century, Henry Parrot, answer this description. Within a few pages of *Wits Recreations* (1640), the popular anthology of epigrams, one finds these titles for English poems: *Similis cum simili. Dulce quod utile, Semel insanivimus, Errantes errare licet.* Yet we should notice that neither in the Greek Anthology nor in Martial was such a practice exemplified; it reflects the usage of the schools. In the second place, as I shall show more explicitly in connection with the work of John Heywood, this writing upon a proverbial theme led to a special variety of epigram, which I have called "proverb-epigrams," in which a proverb or common phrase is quoted and commented upon. These did not originate with Heywood or in England, but it is quite clear that the school-exercise encouraged the growth and spread of this form. Last, writing upon a theme is exemplified in many non-epigrammatic poems of our period, notably in poems by George Gascoigne and other minor lyrists of the late sixteenth century.[8] In *The*

---

[7] Quoted by Foster Watson, *The English Grammar Schools to 1660* (Cambridge, 1908), p. 471.

[8] In *The Paradyse of Dainty Deuises* (1576), there is the well-known lyric by Richard Edwards, *Amantium irae amoris redintegratio est*; com-

Posies (1575), for example, will be found "Gascoigne's Memories," a set of poems upon five themes set the author by five of his friends. Upon the theme *Sat cito, si sat bene* (If it is done well enough, then it is done quickly enough), Gascoigne wrote a sequence of seven sonnets, "therin bewraying his owne *Nimis cito*: and therewith his *Vix bene*." A long poem in the same volume is "The fruites of Warre, written uppon this Theame, *Dulce Bellum inexpertis*." But further examples are unnecessary.

Returning to the schoolroom, we may be sure that often the set theme gave rise to no flash of wit on the part of the boy who puzzled over it. The specimen of composition upon a theme sent home by William Paston, already quoted, is a bit discouraging. And an alumnus of Winchester School, writing in *Notes and Queries* in 1872,[9] gives the following account of a schoolboy's epigram which is almost a *reductio ad absurdum* of the form—an account which will show also that the exercise as we found it prevailing in the sixteenth century persisted down through the eighteenth:

"When I was at Winchester College, nearly eighty years ago, it was the custom of the head master to hear the first class go through their lesson, and then give them a subject on which they were to make an epigram, without having pen or paper, while he went to hear the second class; he then returned to the first class to hear the epigrams they may have made. On one occasion all the boys of the first class gave their epigrams but one; the head master called upon him for his epigram. (The subject given had been 'Femina dux facti.') The boy seemed to hesitate, as if he had not been able to concoct anything like an epigram, and drawled out:

---

pare also Jasper Heywood's "Look or you leap." In *A Gorgious Gallery of Gallant Inuentions* (1578) examples are *Respice finem* and "A proper sonnet, how time consumeth all earthly things." But there are many others.

[9] Fourth series, ix, 465. The same incident is recounted by another contributor, 7th ser., viii (1889), 193-194.

'Femina dux facti. Dux facti femina! Quid tum?
Quid tum! Tum facti femina dux. O.' "

As to the second school-exercise, the imitation or paraphrase of models, we have excellent evidence of its use and
nature in an extant notebook once belonging to a Winchester boy of the mid-sixteenth century.[10] On one page appears
a short Latin disquisition, evidently taken at the master's
dictation, concerning the epigram; it begins, in effect:
"Among all kinds of writing, there is none that tests and
exercises the talents so much as the poem which is usually
called by the special name of *epigram*." It goes on to recommend pointedness and *festivitas*, using the terms *fel*
(gall) and *mel* (honey) probably borrowed from the then
new *Poetices* of Scaliger. An actual assignment appears at
fol. 7ᵛ. The master evidently read to the boys the Greek
epigram (*Anth. Pal.* xi, 226) which runs thus in English:

May the dust lie light on thee when under earth,
wretched Nearchus, so that the dogs may easily drag
thee out.

Then he dictated: "Martial appears to have translated it
thus," and gave the closing couplet of Martial's epigram
ix, 29; "Alciat, thus," giving Alciat's Latin version; "Sleidan
also, thus," with Sleidan's translation. "We have done it this
way," the master went on, and dictated his own rendering;
"now you try your hand." Thus the schoolboy of twelve or
thirteen was set the task of restating the epigram, with four
versions already before him.

How this work with epigrams fitted into the general
training in rhetoric may be seen from a detailed description

---

[10] Add. Ms. 4379. The boy appears to have been William Badger, who
was admitted, at the age of ten, in 1561. His book contains exercises in
Latin verse and prose (most of them doubtless set by Christopher Jonson,
then headmaster) from three of his years at school.

of the teaching of Edmund Campion, the English Jesuit, himself a former Winchester boy, at Prague in 1574:

"In class, he first made the scholars repeat a passage they had learned out of school-hours; then the monitors collected the written exercises, which he looked over and corrected. While he was thus occupied, the boys were trying to imitate a passage of a poet or an orator, which he had set them, or to write a brief account of a garden, a church, a storm, or any other visible object; to vary a sentence in all possible ways; to translate it from one language into another; to write Greek or Latin verses; to convert from one metre into another; to write epigrams, inscriptions, epitaphs; to collect phrases from good authors; to apply the figures of rhetoric to a given subject; or to collect all the topics or commonplaces that are applicable to it."[11]

The assignment "to vary a sentence *in all possible ways*" represents an extension of paraphrasing which was often applied to epigrams. The Greek Anthology itself furnished a suggestion, with its thirty-one epigrams which emphasize, in various ways, the lifelikeness of Myron's statue of a heifer.[12] And among the epigrams which in the sixteenth century still passed as Virgil's there were still better models: here were eleven distichs upon a frozen river, all of them saying merely that where formerly ships sailed now wagons may run;[13] twelve variants of an epigram upon Iris and the

---

[11] Quoted from Simpson's *Life of Campion* by Watson, *English Grammar Schools to 1660*, pp. 105-106.

[12] *Anth. Pal.* IX, 713-742; since there is considerable variety in the details used to make the point, these epigrams are not exactly analogous to the school-exercise. The four epigrams upon the blind man carrying the lame one (*Anth. Pal.* IX, 11-13b) are also pertinent; Sir Thomas More published six Latin versions translated and imitated from these (Cayley, *Memoirs*, II, 281-282).

[13] Quoted and Englished by Richard Stanyhurst, *Thee First Four Bookes of Virgil* (Leyden, 1582; London, 1583, 1620). Stanyhurst questioned the Virgilian authorship. John Penkethman, in *The Epigrams of P. Virgilius Maro* (1624) translated all of the groups of variant epigrams listed in the

rainbow; twelve variant quatrains upon the rising of the sun; twelve variant hexastichs concerning the signs of the zodiac; and thirteen variants of a quatrain upon the four seasons of the year. To what lengths the exercise in multiple paraphrase might be carried, we learn from an examination of John Stockwood's *Progymnasma Scholasticum* (1597), an important school textbook. John Brinsley recommended Stockwood in these words:

. . . "For turning of Verses divers ways, M. Stockwood his *Progymnasmata* (sic) *Scholasticum* is *instar omnium,* to direct and incourage young scholars. In which booke towards the end of it, you shall have one Disticke or couple of Verses, varied 450 ways."[14]

The poem upon which Stockwood exercised so much ingenuity is *Anth. Pal.* v, 224, by Macedonius Consul, which runs in English:

> Cease, Love, to aim at my heart and liver, and if thou must shoot, let it be at some other part of me.

Stockwood's versions begin:

~~~~~~~~~

text. He himself wrote an additional Latin distich upon the frozen river, in order to make that series an even twelve in number. In his preface, Penkethman notes the possibility of non-Virgilian authorship, saying that the greater number of the epigrams may "haue issued (as *Scaliger* and other Commentators conceiue) from the learned heads of more ancient Poets."

It is pertinent to the subject of this chapter that along with Martial, Ausonius, and the Greek Anthology, the schoolboy would think of Virgil as an important writer of epigrams. In Donatus's life of Virgil, regularly prefixed to editions of his poems, there were three epigrams supposed to be his (see below, pp. 157-163); and further, in most editions of the *opera* published before 1600 and many thereafter, there was a considerable group of epigrams included in an appendix—practically all of them now assigned to non-Virgilian authorship. We shall meet with the use of these in connection with the work of Nicholas Grimald, Henry Parker, George Chapman, and others.

[14] *Ludus Literarius* (1612, 1627), reprinted (Liverpool and London, 1917), p. 197.

Linque Cupido iecur: cordi quoque parcito si vis
Figere, fige alio tela cruenta loco.

Parce meo iecori; intactum mihi linquite pectus:
Omnia de reliquo corpore membra pete.

It should be added that immediately before this series of
four hundred and fifty variants, Stockwood printed his one
hundred and five renderings of the last two lines of *Anth.
Pal.* VI, 76, an epigram by Agathias Scholasticus concerning
Anchises.

Stockwood's textbook deserves further attention. It was
a collection of seventy-five Greek epigrams, a selection made
from those already culled from the Greek Anthology and
edited by Henri Étienne (Henricus Stephanus, "Henry
Stephens"), surrounded with copious aids to the student.
Foster Watson's detailed description may be quoted:

". . . A full vocabulary and commentary is given of each
Greek word that presents any difficulty, and a word for word
translation is given of the Greek into Latin, and alternative
verse-renderings in Latin are presented to the pupil. Wher-
ever Stockwood can find them he gives interpretations in
Latin from well-known Latinists, such as Sir Thomas More,
Erasmus, Politian, Marcellus, Alciat, Sleidan. Usually there
is given the Latin rendering of H. Stephens, and always
that of Stockwood himself. Often after giving one of his
own, he will offer one or two more *aliter ab eodem* until he
produces the masterpiece of 450 variants of his own. He says
he was provoked to do this *tour de force* by the example of
Stephens so as to give courage to Grammar-school boys and
studious youth that they might try to do the same with other
epigrams in their leisure hours, an employment which he
promises will lead to their great delight, and at the same
time be of high usefulness to them."[15]

_____

[15] *Op. cit.*, pp. 484-485.

But there was another exercise in varying verses which, while it cannot have been a very important one in the schools, is represented in Stockwood and elsewhere. This consists of rearranging the actual words of a verse without altering the meter or the sense. Thus Stockwood printed one hundred and four arrangements of the line,

> Est mea spes Christus solus, qui de cruce pendet.

A verse so written and varied is to be called, according to Scaliger, *Proteus*. We must notice the work in this kind of Bernard Bauhuis, a French Jesuit, whose monostich in honor of the Virgin Mary is perhaps the most famous Protean line in literature; it reads, in its original order of words,

> Tot sibi sunt dotes, Virgo, quot sidera coelo.

Bauhuis included this verse, under the title of *Proteus parthenicus* in his popular *Epigrammatum libri 9* (Antwerp, 1615, 1619, 1620, etc.) with the statement that 1022 arrangements might be made of the words without impairing either sense or meter. And in 1617 there was issued from the press at Antwerp a book by Henry Dupuy (Erycius Puteanus) giving the 1022 variants. To this book, *Pietatis Thaumata in Proteum parthenicum unius libri versum, et unius versus librum*, Robert Burton alluded in the *Anatomy of Melancholy* when he wrote (II, ii, iv):

"... And rather than do nothing, vary a verse a thousand waies with Putean, so torturing his wits, or as Rainnerus of Luneburge, 2,150 times in his 'Proteus Poeticus,' or Scaliger, Chrysolithus, Cleppisus, and others have in like sort done."

Mathematics came to the aid of literature, and P. Prestet demonstrated that the words of *Proteus parthenicus* were capable of 3376 combinations, all in good meter; while another mathematician, Jacques Bernoulli, showed that if meter was disregarded, the words would combine in 40,327 ways. We may add that Bauhuis wrote another Protean verse,

Rex, Dux, Sol, Lex, Lux, Fons, Spes, Pax, Mons,
Petra, Christus,

which he asserted would admit of 3,628,800 arrangements.

≺ III ≻

THIS leads us to the consideration of some other *tours de force* which were practised in connection with epigram-writing, both in the schools and outside. Scaliger solemnly discusses them, and under his authority school-masters and scholars "rather than do nothing" produced them.[16] Anyone reading collections of epigrams, epitaphs, posies, or other sorts of poetic trifles, is continually coming upon those which involve acrostics, telestichs, or anagrams, or in some other manner display the ingenuity of the author. Some are written so as to make a certain pattern on the page; others are chronograms (or eteostichs), in which capitalized letters give a notable date. We shall find specimens of these "difficult trifles" in English, but they are more numerous among the poems of those who wrote in Latin; for the variable word order of Latin is an aid to the writer. Martial protested against ingenious distortions in his day:

"Because I do not pride myself on topsy-turvy verses, nor read backwards in obscene Sotadics; because nowhere does a Greekling echo answer you, . . . I am not, Classicus, a bad poet after all. . . . 'Tis degrading to undertake difficult trifles; and foolish is the labor spent on puerilities."[17]

~~~~~~~~~~

[16] Again, there were precedents in the Greek Anthology and in the work of mediaeval, if not classical, Latin authors.

[17] II, 86, translated by Ker. Lines 9-10 of the epigram were often quoted by writers of the Renaissance:
    turpe est difficiles habere nugas
    et stultus labor est ineptiarum.

Ben Jonson echoed Martial's satire in vigorous English couplets. Yet as late as 1650 we find Thomas Hobbes writing: "In an epigram or a sonnet a man may vary his measures, and seek glory from a needless difficulty, as he that contrived verses into the forms of an organ, a hatchet, an egg, an altar, and a pair of wings."[18] Readers familiar with *The Arte of English Poesie* (1589) will recall the pages of instruction therein for poets who "seek glory from a needless difficulty." The author was merely applying to English verse a few of the many devices which had been practised by writers in Latin.

It is noteworthy also that in the chapter upon the epigram, in the book just cited, one of the two epigrams given as specimens is an example of ingenuity rather than of wit. The story which forms the setting comes from Donatus's life of Virgil,[19] wherein is recounted how Virgil, having posted at the palace gate of Augustus a distich which pleased the emperor, was too modest to sign or to acknowledge the poem. Another author proceeded to claim it. In the words of *The Arte of English Poesie* the story proceeds:

". . . Whereupon *Virgill* seing himself by his ouermuch modestie defrauded of the reward, that an im-

[18] In "The Answer of Mr. Hobbes to Sir William Davenant's preface before *Gondibert*," printed with Davenant's *Gondibert*.

[19] See above, p. 153, n. The life by Aelius Donatus, a grammarian of the fourth century A.D., is supposed to have been a sober and fairly authentic account, but to have suffered corruption by mediaeval additions; so that a writer in the *Nouvelle Biographie Générale* could refer to it as 'une mauvaise compilation, pleine d'anecdotes puériles.' Donatus first appeared in English as a part of Twyne's additions to Phaer's translation of the *Aeneid*, edition of 1573. Virgil's distich upon Augustus, supposed to have been occasioned by the appearance of fair weather for the imperial games, follows:

> Nocte pluit tota, redeunt spectacula mane:
> Diuium imperium cum Ioue Caesar habet.

('All night it rains; the shows are resumed in the morning: Caesar holds a sway shared with Jove.')

pudent had gotten by abuse of his merit, came the next
night, and fastened vpon the same place this halfe
metre, foure times iterated. Thus.

> *Sic vos non vobis*
> *Sic vos non vobis*
> *Sic vos non vobis*
> *Sic vos non vobis*

"And there it remained a great while because no
man wist what it meant, till *Virgill* opened the
whole fraud by this deuise. He wrote aboue the
same halfe metres this whole verse *Exameter*.

> *Hos ego versiculos feci tulit alter honores.*

And then finished the foure half metres, thus.

> *Sic vos non vobis*   *Fertis aratra boues*
> *Sic vos non vobis*   *Vellera fertis oues*
> *Sic vos non vobis*   *Mellificatis apes*
> *Sic vos non vobis*   *Nidificatis aues.*

And put to his name *Publius Virgilius Maro*. This
matter came by and by to Th'emperours eare, who
taking great pleasure in the deuise called for *Virgill*, and gaue him not onely a present reward, etc."[20]

---

[20] Arber's reprint (1869), pp. 69-70, correcting *Indificatis* to *Nidificatis*.
Penkethman translated the single hexameter,

> I these Verses did compose,
> But the praise another chose,

and the epigram,

> So you, not for you, Birds knit slender peeces,
> So you, not for you, Cattell weare your fleeces,
> So you, not for you, Bees your Sweet prepare,
> So you, not for you, Oxen draw the share.

The translation is not very clear; the point is, of course, that sheep (addressed directly) bear fleeces, but do not reap the benefit, oxen draw
ploughs, not for themselves but for others, and so on.

For other references to this epigram and its story, see Emma M. Denkinger, "Some Renaissance References to *Sic vos non vobis*," *Philological
Quarterly*, x (1931), 151-162. Miss Denkinger does not discuss the story
as told in *The Arte of English Poesie*.

Another *schema*, which might be used to gain epigrammatic compression, was that called by Scaliger *versus concordantes*, thus exemplified (*Poetices*, II, xxx):

$$\left.\begin{array}{l}\text{Et canis}\\\text{Et lupus}\end{array}\right\}\text{in syluis}\left\{\begin{array}{l}\text{venatur}\\\text{nutritur}\end{array}\right\}\&\text{ omnis}\left\{\begin{array}{l}\text{seruat}\\\text{uastat.}\end{array}\right.$$

The compilers of *A Helpe to Discourse* (12th edition, 1636)
found the aphorism worthy of translation:

	Dog		hunts		keepeth
The		in the woods		and al things	
	Wolfe		is nourished		destroieth.

It should be pointed out that such a pattern merely presents
graphically certain parallelisms of words or sounds which
might occur in rhetorical prose as well as in verse; some
Euphuistic sentences could be printed as *versus concordantes*.
The following, from a sermon by Elinand, will illustrate:

Quaesivit me diabolus, et invenit, et circumvenit;
quaesivit me Christus, invenit et subvenit.[21]

Written as *versus concordantes*, this gives:

	diabolus, et		circum-	
Quaesivit me		invenit et		venit.
	Christus		sub-	

These *versus concordantes* had some vogue as inscriptions
on tombs, possibly because they allow of economy in the
number of words to be chiseled.[22] A specimen which turns
up again and again in miscellanies and collections may be

21 Quoted by C. S. Baldwin, *Mediaeval Rhetoric and Poetic* (New York,
1928), p. 253, as an example of how a prose-epigram might be pointed
with rime. Elinand, or Helinand, was a French poet and homilist of the
twelfth century.

22 T. F. Ravenshaw, *Antiente Epitaphes* (1878), records several examples
from tombs of the sixteenth and seventeenth centuries.

quoted as found by John Weever inscribed upon a table in St. Anne's Church, Aldersgate:[23]

Qu	an	tris	di	c	vul	stra
	os	guis	ti	ro	um	nere	uit.
H	san	Chris	mi	t	mu	la

The English writer of the sixteenth century who furnished the greatest number and variety of these *tours de force* was Richard Willes, who, after a training in Latin versification at Winchester, proceeded to New College, but later left England, became a Jesuit, and taught rhetoric in Perugia. In 1574, having returned to England, he renounced his Roman Catholic faith; and he seems to have done considerable miscellaneous writing. His earliest book, *Poematum Liber* (1573) contains specimens of nearly every sort of versified ingenuity, including poems in the form of an altar, a sword, pyramids, and wings.[24] Willes composed one verse of a very rare variety, the palindrome, which reads the same when taken, letter by letter, either backward or forward:

Tara sibi svbito dotibvs ibis arat.

[23] *Antient Funeral Monuments* (1631), p. 391. Stow, in *A Survay of London* (1598, p. 246, wrongly numbered 446), found them 'on an olde stone' in the church of St. Olaf in Aldersgate. The verses may be translated, "Those whom the serpent has overthrown, sadly and severely wounded, the blood of Christ by marvellous grace has cleansed."

Abraham Fraunce quotes these lines as "those olde ones," in his *Arcadian Rhetorike* (1588). In *A Helpe to Discourse* (12th ed., 1636), p. 35, a variant is printed, with an English translation. The Latin lines, with some changes, were printed by Beloe in *The Sexagenarian* (1817), II, 311, under the heading, "Copied from Porson's Manuscript, but whether his own or not is uncertain."

[24] It should be recorded that the author also exemplifies the more usual species, such as the ode, the psalm, the hymn, the encomium, the elegy, the epitaph. In all, the collection contains one hundred poems, each of a different sort; it is plainly intended for the academic audience, with a complete set of *scholia* by the author himself. It is, in fact, addressed on the title page to the scholars of Winchester College.

But the poet does not provide a translation. In one quatrain he uses all of the letters of the alphabet in each distich. In the following, he has included all of the parts of speech in each line:

> *Hosp.* Hem, sed in his studijs, nimium defesse,
> laboras?
> *Po.* Proh, quia cum studijs non tibi nata meto?

> (Visitor: "Ha, but are you toiling at these studies,
> over-tired one?"

> Poet: "Alas, yes, for amid my studies do I not
> harvest a crop for you?")

A scheme of word arrangement we have not hitherto discussed is that exemplified by Willes's distich entitled *Dum Orator diceret* (While the orator speaks). Such a poem is called, according to Scaliger and Willes's own scholium, *carmen correlativum,* "because all of the words have reference to each other respectively, and match in an exact order."

> Horrida, lecta, graues: effata, vocabula, gestus:
> Orno, loquor, signo: schemate, voce, manu.

Literally, this is to be translated: "Blunt, polished, weighty; propositions, words, gestures; I adorn, I speak, I render; with figure, with voice, with hand." By matching the respective words of each group, we have the orator saying: "I adorn blunt propositions with figures, I speak polished words with my voice, I make weighty gestures with my hand."[25] This method of obtaining compression of thought was current throughout our period, in non-epigrammatic poetry as well

---

[25] If we may suppose the poem to be directed at an orator who was faulty only in gesture, then there is a satirical point in the use of *graues,* which should be translated "ponderous" or "wearisome."

as in epigrams. A specimen from the latter part of the six-teenth century appears in *Harl. Ms.* 7392; the Latin original is Scaliger's example of *carmen correlativum*:

> Pastor, arator, eques, paui, colui, superaui,
> capras, rus, hostes, fronde, ligone, manu.[26]

Two translations follow in the manuscript, the first signed by Saintlowe Knyvestonne, who perhaps is responsible also for the second:

I sheppard	I plowman	I horseman light
Have fedd	have plowed	have put to flight
My goates	my grownde	my foes in feild
W^th bowes	wth plowes	with speare & sheild.
A hearde	a swaine	a noble knight
I fed	I tild	I did subdue
My goates	my growndes	my foes by flighte
W^th bowes	with plowes	these hands then slue.

By reading downward instead of across, the related phrases are brought together.

Abraham Fraunce also cites the Latin verses, without giving a name to the device of them, saying they 'bee aswell knowne, as their author is vnknowne.' He translates them thus:

> A goteheard, plowman, knight, my goates, my fields, my foes,
> I fed, I tild, I kild, with bowes, with plowes, with blowes,

and follows with two versions in French.[27]

This poem, too, appears in the Virgilian appendix, as printed in many early editions of Virgil. It is there as a part

---

[26] Scaliger had found it among the poems ascribed to Pentadius.
[27] *The Arcadian Rhetorike* (1588?), E1^v.

of a group of distichs representing epitaphs, or an epitaph, upon Virgil as written by himself. The first distich of the group is the well-known epitaph which Donatus ascribes to Virgil's own hand:

> Mantua me genuit: Calabri rapuere: tenet nunc
>   Parthenope. cecini pascua, rura, duces.

> (Mantua bore me, the Calabrians took me, now Parthenope holds me. I have sung flocks, fields, princes.)

The last three words of this epitaph suggest the connection with Pentadius' distich, which would be interpreted as referring to Virgil's having impersonated a shepherd (in the *Eclogues*), a farmer (in the *Georgics*), and a knight or warrior (in the *Aeneid*).

Sometimes the corresponding words were numbered, giving, as in Sidney's *Arcadia*:

> Vertue Bewty and Speeche, did stryke, wounde,
>   Charme,
> My Hart, Eyes, Eares with wonder, Love, De-
>   lighte
> First, Second Last did bynde, enforce and Arme,
> His worckes Shewes Fruites wth witt, grace and
>   vowes might.[28]

A very popular lyric, attributable upon good authority to Sir Walter Ralegh, follows this pattern throughout:

---

[28] *The Countess of Pembroke's Arcadia, Being the Original Version*, ed. Albert Feuillerat (Cambridge, 1926), p. 216. The quotation represents the first four lines of a sonnet, the whole of it being in "correlative verses"; the whole is given by Fraunce, *loc. cit.*

Her face, her tongue, her wit, so fair, so sweet, so
sharp,
First bent, then drew, now hit, mine eye, mine ear,
my heart:
Mine eye, mine ear, my heart, to like, to learn, to
love,
Her face, her tongue, her wit, doth lead, doth teach,
doth move:
Her face, her tongue, her wit, with beams, with
sound, with art,
Doth blind, doth charm, doth rule, mine eye, mine
ear, my heart.[29]

Finally, we should notice this example from Edmund Spenser (*Faerie Queene*, II, iv, 35), wherein *carmen correlativum* has set the pattern for a stanza, a pattern which Spenser manages to make more flexible than did Sidney and Ralegh in the poems just quoted:

Wrath, gealosie, griefe, love, do thus expell:
Wrath is a fire; and gealosie a weede;
Griefe is a flood; and love a monster fell;
The fire of sparkes, the weede of little seede,
The flood of drops, the Monster filth did breede:
But sparks, seed, drops, and filth, do thus delay;
The sparks soone quench, the springing seed out-
weed,
The drops dry up, and filth wipe cleane away:
So shall wrath, gealosy, griefe, love, die and decay.[30]

～～～～～～～

[29] Called "A Reporting Sonnet" in early editions of Davison's *Poetical Rhapsody* (1602); in later editions, "In the Grace of Wit, of Tongue, and Face." A variant had appeared earlier in *The Phoenix Nest* (1593). I quote from Hannah, *Poems of Sir Walter Raleigh* (1892), p. 15, the first of two stanzas.

[30] This stanza also was cited as a specimen of *carmen correlativum* (though not so denominated) by Abraham Fraunce in *The Arcadian Rhetorike*, fol. E₃ʳ.

Without accumulating further evidence, we can say that a poet had always at his disposal this device for gaining sententious compression, and that many poets used it.[31]

Another author who treated of "conceited verses" was Abraham Fraunce, whose *Arcadian Rhetorike* draws copiously upon Willes and Scaliger. In common with those authors, he discusses *versus recurrentes*, or verses whose words give a meaning when read backward, usually the opposite meaning from their original one. We have seen an instance (above, p. 119) in the popular story about George Buchanan.[32] We may quote another example from Fraunce:

---

[31] A. M. Witherspoon, *The Influence of Robert Garnier on Elizabethan Drama* (New Haven, 1924), notes (p. 175) in Garnier's plays and the English plays influenced by them "the custom of using a series of words in the same construction to form a line of poetry." He does not relate this custom to *carmen correlativum*, though some of his examples are perfect specimens. These lines are from *Croesus* (1604) by Sir William Alexander:

Grief, rage, spite, shame, amazement, and despaire,
Gall'd, toss'd, burn'd, dash'd, astonish'd, and destroy'd.
(II. 997-998)

Some rag'd, some groan'd, some sigh'd, roar'd,
promis'd, pray'd,
As blows, falls, faintnesse, paine, hope, anguish, mov'd.
(II. 2557-2558)

By relaxing the strictness of correspondence among words, a writer may get such a result as this from Brandon's *Octavia* (1598), II. 1045-1046:

I heare, I see, I know, I feele, I finde,
The shamefull wrong, the scorne and high disdaine.

There are examples, some with strict correspondence and some without it, in Garnier's French dramas. In English literature, the most famous lines which seem to have been influenced by this rhetorical device are in *Paradise Lost* (ii, 947-949):

. . . the Fiend
O'er bog or steep, through strait, rough, dense, or rare,
With head, hands, wings, or feet, pursues his way.

[32] Fraunce quotes the distich there attributed to Buchanan as by "Philelphus of Pope Pius." (Francesco Fidelfo, 1398-1481, one of the most learned of Italian Humanists, is as likely an author for it as anyone.) He goes on: "Who so desireth to see more of this kinde, let him read *Accords Bizarrures*, and *Scaligers* books *de arte Poetica*."

[165]

... "I had almost forgotten an other olde verse, inferior to none of the rest, it is this.

> *Sacrum pingue dabo, nec macrum sacrificabo,*

Saith *Cain*, in an Hexameter; which (if you reade it backward) will make *Abels* answer in a Pentameter, thus:

> *Sacrificabo macrum, nec dabo pingue sacrum.*"[33]

Fraunce himself worked at confecting verbal ingenuities, as may be seen in his *Lawiers Logike* (1588) and elsewhere.[34] We may contemplate his eight lines incorporating the motto *Vive vale* in four ways:

> *V*ires *I*n *V*erbis *E*t *V*ocibus *A*rte Latent*E*
> *I*nque foro vires et vires ante tribuna*L*
> *V*ires in sophia, recta ratione docend*A*
> *E*nthea multiplici profert dialectica fruct*V*
> *V*erba dat eximia, sed verba fluentia leg*E*
> *A*rdua divino depromit dogmata sens*V*
> *L*aetentur populi logices laetentur alumn*I*
> *E*n Lux *A*lma Viris *E*n *V*icta *I*ura tumult*V*.

◄ IV ►

If it has seemed, in the earlier part of this chapter, that Winchester College looms large in our story, that impression is justified by the evident fact that epigram-writing has played a larger part in the discipline of that school than elsewhere. Timothe Kendall and Sir John Harington gained their interest in this kind of poetry at Eton, but a large number of the

---

[33] It will be observed that he mixes the names of the speakers. It should be Abel who says: "I will give a rich offering, nor will I sacrifice a meagre thing."

[34] A number of his *tours de force* were reprinted by G. C. Moore Smith in the Introduction to his edition (Louvain, 1906) of Fraunce's Latin comedy, *Victoria*. It should also be noted that Fraunce wrote an entire work on the impresa, or device.

principal epigrammatists of the Elizabethan period were Wykehamists, notably John Owen, Sir John Davies, Thomas Bastard, John Hoskins, and John Heath. The headmastership of Christopher Jonson, from 1560 to 1571, probably stimulated Latin verse-composition, if any stimulation was needed. Jonson himself wrote a series of epigrams, published with Willes's *Poematum Liber* (1573), upon all of the former headmasters of the College.[35] It was under the headmastership of his successor, Thomas Bilson, that the men just named studied epigram-writing. Bilson, who later became Bishop of Worcester, Bishop of Winchester, and Privy Councillor of King James, had gained some reputation as a Latin poet and, according to Anthony à Wood, left a collection of *carmina* in manuscript. Bilson's interest in word play is evident from his published prose.

We have three early collections of schoolboy verse from Winchester, all occasioned by royal visits.[36] The first (Royal Ms. 12 A xxxiii) celebrates a visitation by young Edward VI in 1552; it contains poems by forty-three boys, among whom was Thomas Stapleton (who wrote the only Greek poetry in the volume), later the Catholic biographer of Sir Thomas More. The second collection (Rawlinson Poetical Ms. 187) is a beautifully written volume entitled *Carmina Scholae Wichamicae ad Elisabetham Angliae Reginam*, evidently prepared for presentation to the Queen upon a visit.[37] Of the

~~~~~~~~~

[35] A number of his distichs are quoted and translated in A. F. Leach's *History of Winchester College* (1899), pp. 278, 284, 289-291. While a schoolboy, Jonson wrote a long poem recounting the duties and pleasures of one day's life at Winchester.

[36] There are also such collections made by Eton scholars. King's Ms. 12, A. lxv is a volume which was prepared and given to Queen Elizabeth as a New Year's gift at the beginning of the year 1560. King's Ms. 12, A. xxx is a similar book presented to the Queen in 1563, when she moved from Westminster to Windsor on account of the plague.

[37] In 1570, according to Leach in his *History*, p. 290, but this date is hard to reconcile with the fact that several of the contributors were not elected scholars until 1572—and admission might be as much as a year

eleven boys whose verses are there preserved, only John Pits appears to have achieved any fame; like Stapleton, he became a Catholic exile; his chief work, *De Illustribus Angliae Scriptoribus* (1619), is of doubtful value because of its continual borrowing from Bale's earlier catalogue of authors. It is a Winchester tradition that when Queen Elizabeth saw, at Winchester, the picture of the "Bibling-rod" on the wall of the schoolroom, she asked one of the boys whether he was familiar with the subject of the picture. He replied with a line of Virgil:

> Infandum, Regina, jubes renovare dolorem.

> (You bid me, O Queen, renew an unutterable grief.)

The third collection I have mentioned (Tanner Ms. 466, fols. 40-57) includes, without authors' names, the verses made in honor of a visit of Prince Charles in August, 1618. A few of the poems are in Greek; three are chronograms, working in the letters which give the date, and several are based upon anagrams, or rearrangements of the letters of Charles's name. In fact, comparison with the other two collections shows that here there is a greater preponderance of brief epigrams (since the earlier volumes included sapphic odes and other forms), and that verbal ingenuity is more strongly emphasized in this later group of poems.

We have already recounted some epigrammatic incidents in Winchester's history. Another one is preserved in Harleian Ms. 7332 (fol. 19ʳ), under the title "An extempore verse upon the Instability of fortune by a boy at Winton":

> Hic est hic non est hic non fuit hic fuit
> O brave cry'd the usher, wᶜʰ made out the verse &
> the boy sat downe and thank'd him.

---

later than election. Perhaps Leach is referring to a different visitation from that celebrated by Rawl. Poet. Ms. 187.

A scansion will show that "Oh, brave!" gives the spondee which is necessary to fill out the boy's hexameter. Most Winchester boys went up to New College, Oxford—all of the Wykehamist writers named previously did so except Sir John Davies, who went to Queen's College. And from New College also come incidents involving epigrams. One of the cleverest of all specimens of bilingual punning grew out of the death of a member of New College, Payne by name, under the wardenship of Dr. Martin Culpepper, who seems to have been universally disliked:

"D^r. Culpepper beinge warden of Newe colledge in Oxon: and much disliked by the fellowes thereof: one M^r. Payne dyinge generally beloued of all the society, and accordinge to ye vse of scholars of ye howse clappinge verses about the wall of the colledge cloysters one amongst the rest to sheawe howe much beloued of them all, M^r. Payne was & howe much dislyked D^r. Culpepper was: sett up in the cloyster this one verse followinge

Poena tolli potest, Culpa perennis erit."[38]

As it stands, and as Dr. Culpepper might read it on his morning's walk in the cloister, this is merely a line of Ovid.[39] But to the ear attuned for them, the names Payne and Culpepper sound out, with the implication that while Payne has unfortunately passed away, Culpepper will go on forever.

---

[38] Tanner Ms. 169, fol. 76^v, where it is signed by Francis Davison, 2 September, 1609; the incident belongs, however, to the period about 1580. It is told also in Rawlinson Poet. Ms. 117, fol. 174^v, and Add. Ms. 15,227, fol. 20^v.

[39] *Epistola ex Ponto*, I, i, 64. The line actually reads, in modern editions,
Poena potest demi, culpa perennis erit.
but in either reading the meaning is: "Punishment can be remitted, but the guilt will be eternal."